Vanna's AFGHANS
ALL THROUGH THE HOUSE

Compiled and Edited by
Janica York

Oxmoor House®

©1997 by Oxmoor House, Inc.
Book Division of Southern Progress Corporation
P.O. Box 2463, Birmingham, Alabama 35201

Published by Oxmoor House, Inc., and Leisure
Arts, Inc.

Library of Congress Catalog Number: 96-72549
Hardcover ISBN: 0-8487-1549-7
Softcover ISBN: 0-8487-1602-7
Manufactured in the United States of America
First Printing 1997

Editor-in-Chief: Nancy Fitzpatrick Wyatt
Senior Crafts Editor: Susan Ramey Cleveland
Senior Editor, Editorial Services: Olivia Kindig Wells
Art Director: James Boone

Vanna's Afghans All Through the House

Editor: Janica Lynn York
Editorial Assistant: Barzella Estle
Copy Editor: L. Amanda Owens
Photographers: Ralph Anderson, Keith Harrelson
Photo Stylists: Katie Stoddard, Linda Baltzell Wright
Associate Art Director: Cynthia R. Cooper
Senior Designer: Larry Hunter
Illustrators: Barbara Ball, Anita Bice, Kelly Davis
Production and Distribution Director: Phillip Lee
Associate Production Manager: Theresa L. Beste
Publishing Systems Administrator: Rick Tucker

We're Here for You!
We at Oxmoor House are dedicated to serving you
with reliable information that expands your imagi-
nation and enriches your life. We welcome your
comments and suggestions. Please write to us at:
    Oxmoor House
    Editor, *Vanna's Afghans All Through the House*
    2100 Lakeshore Drive
    Birmingham, AL 35209
To order additional publications,
call 1-205-877-6560.

Contents

Vertical Ripple on page 96

Playful Primaries on page 42

Windowpanes on page 12

Wheels of Popcorn on page 46

Crochet is one of the most relaxing and enjoyable hobbies I've found. I'm so eager to share the joys of this time-honored craft with you that I didn't hesitate when Lion Brand Yarn Company, Oxmoor House, and Leisure Arts approached me about doing this book. After the fun and the excitement of working on my first crochet book, *Vanna's Afghans A to Z,* I was thrilled to start another publishing venture.

David Blumenthal, senior vice president of Lion Brand Yarn Company, challenged top designers across the country to submit their best creations. After looking through dozens and dozens of swatches and sketches, we chose our favorites—a terrific collection of over sixty afghans and other crocheted projects.

Stitched in Lion Brand's fashionable colors, patterns range from fresh to familiar. From cuddly baby blankets to romantic feminine throws to sturdy bold afghans,

we've included designs for everyone and every room in the house. In fact, you can see how afghans decorate *my* home in many of the photographs!

With an active toddler and a busy taping schedule for "Wheel of Fortune," I like projects I can stitch quickly. But I also enjoy the challenging heirloom patterns. You'll find both in this book.

Whichever projects you choose to make, I know you'll appreciate the clear directions and large color photographs. If you're a beginner (or if you just need a refresher), be sure to refer to the General Directions at the back of the book.

I hope you enjoy this great collection of exciting crochet patterns as much as I do.

Vanna

I'm happy to recommend a couple of fast and easy afghans: *Buffalo Checks* (page 41) and *Great Gingham* (page 134).

If you have a little more free time, create an heirloom afghan with *Tyrolean Christmas* (page 66) or *Aran Fisherman* (page 98).

Clusters and Lace

Take a moment to relax with a cup of tea and a snuggly afghan. A lacy border surrounds the soft texture of cluster stitches.

Materials
Chunky-weight brushed
acrylic yarn, approximately:
42 oz. (1,890 yd.) green
Size J crochet hook or size to
obtain gauge

Finished Size
Approximately 43" x 59"

Gauge
In pat, 3 cl and 6 rows = 4"

Pattern Stitches
Cl: (Yo, insert hook in st or sp
indicated, yo and pull up lp, yo
and pull through 2 lps) 4 times, yo
and pull through all 5 lps on
hook.

Tr-cl: * Yo twice, insert hook in
next st, yo and pull up lp, (yo and
pull through 2 lps) twice; rep
from * twice, yo and pull through
all 4 lps on hook.

Ch 110.

Row 1 (ws): Sc in 2nd ch from
hook, ch 3, sk 1 ch, cl in next ch,
ch 1, * sk 1 ch, sc in next ch, ch 3,
sk 1 ch, cl in next ch, ch 1; rep
from * across to last 3 sc, sc in last
sc: 27 cl.

Row 2 (rs): Ch 5, turn; sk first sc
and ch-1 sp, sc in top of cl, ch 3,
cl in next ch-3 sp, * ch 1, sk next
sc and ch-1 sp, sc in top of cl, ch 3,
cl in next ch-3 sp; rep from * across
to last sc, ch 1, dc in last sc: 27 cl.

Row 3: Ch 1, turn; sk first dc,
sc in top of cl, ch 3, cl in next
ch-3 sp, * ch 1, sk next sc and
ch-1 sp, sc in top of cl, ch 3, cl in
next ch-3 sp; rep from * across to
last ch-5 sp, ch 2, sk next sc, sc in
next ch-5 sp.

Row 4: Ch 5, turn; sk first sc and
ch-2 sp, sc in top of cl, ch 3, cl in
next ch-3 sp, * ch 1, sk next sc and
ch-1 sp, sc in top of cl, ch 3, cl in
next ch-3 sp; rep from * across to
last sc, ch 1, dc in last sc.

Rep rows 3 and 4 alternately
until piece measures approximately 51", ending with row 3.
Last Row: Ch 5, turn; * sc in first
ch-3 sp, ch 3; rep from * across to
last ch-1 sp, sl st in last ch-1 sp; do
not fasten off.

Border
Rnd 1 (rs): With rs facing, ch 1,
sc in same st, * work 129 sc evenly
across to next corner, 3 sc in corner, work 93 sc evenly across to
next corner, 3 sc in corner; rep
from * around; do not join.
Rnd 2: * Ch 3, sk 3 sc, (dc in next
6 sc, ch 3, sk 3 sc) across to corner, 2 dc in last sc of side, 2 dc in
corner dc, 2 dc in first sc of next
side; rep from * around; do not
join.
Rnd 3: Sc in first ch-3 sp, ch 5,
(tr-cl beg in next dc, ch 5) twice,
sc in next ch-3 sp, ch 5, (tr-cl beg
in next dc, ch 5) twice; rep from *
around; join with sl st to beg sc.
Rnd 4: Sl st in first 5 chs and in
first tr-cl, sl st in ch-5 sp, ch 4,
11 tr in same ch-5 sp, * ch 3,
sk next 2 ch-5 sps, 12 tr in next
ch-5 sp; rep from * around, ch 4;
join with sl st to top of beg ch-4;
fasten off.

Project was stitched with Jiffy: Country Green #181.

Petal Soft

This fluffy white throw adds tranquil elegance to any setting. Work stitches in the back loops only to create the gently puffed petals.

Materials
Chunky-weight brushed acrylic yarn, approximately:
33 oz. (1,485 yd.) white
Size K crochet hook or size to obtain gauge

Finished Size
Approximately 39" x 39"

Gauge
Ea Square = 11"

Square (Make 9.)

Center
Ch 4, join with sl st to form ring.
Rnd 1 (rs): Ch 1, 8 sc in ring, join with sl st to beg sc.
Note: Mark last rnd as rs.
Rnd 2: Ch 2 [counts as hdc], hdc in same st, 2 hdc in next sc and in ea sc around; join with sl st in top of beg ch-2: 16 hdc.
Rnd 3: Ch 3 [counts as dc], dc in same st, 2 dc in next hdc and in ea hdc around; join with sl st in top of beg ch-3: 32 dc.
Rnd 4: Ch 1, sc in same st, sc in next dc, * hdc in next dc, dc in next dc, (dc, 3 tr, dc) in next dc [corner made], dc in next dc, hdc in next dc **, sc in next 3 dc; rep from * around, ending last rep at **, sc in last dc; join with sl st to beg sc.
Rnd 5: Ch 1, sc in same st, sc in next 5 sts, 3 sc in corner tr, * sc in next 11 sts, 3 sc in corner tr; rep from * twice, sc in next 5 sts; join

with sl st to beg sc: 56 sc; fasten off.
Note: Mark ea corner sc.

Petal
Row 1 (rs): With rs facing, join yarn in 6th sc from corner sc, ch 1, sc in same sc, sc in next 3 sc.
Row 2 (ws): Ch 1, turn; working in ft lps only, sc in next 4 sc, sc in both lps of next sc on rnd 5: 5 sc.
Row 3: Ch 1, turn; working in bk lps only, sc in ea sc on prev row, sc in end of prev row, sc in both lps of next sc on rnd 5: 7 sc.
Row 4: Ch 1, turn; working in ft lps only, sc in ea sc on prev row, sc in end of prev row, sc in both lps of next sc on rnd 5: 9 sc.
Rows 5–11: Rep rows 3 and 4 alternately, ending with row 3: 23 sc; fasten off, leaving 6" tail. Mark 12th sc as corner.

Rep rows 1–11 for ea rem Petal. Thread yarn needle with 6" tail and sew Petals tog at base.

Edging
Rnd 1 (rs): With rs facing, join yarn with sl st in any corner, ch 3, dc in same st, working in bk lps only, work 20 dc evenly sp across to next corner, * 2 dc in corner, work 20 dc evenly sp across to next corner; rep from * around; join with sl st to top of beg ch-3.
Rnd 2: Ch 3, 2 dc in same st, working in both lps, dc in ea dc across to corner, * 3 dc in corner, dc in ea dc across to corner; rep from * around; join with sl st to top of beg ch-3; fasten off.

Assembly
Afghan is 3 squares wide and 3 squares long. Whipstitch squares tog.

Border
Rnd 1 (rs): With rs facing, join yarn with sl st in corner, ch 1, sc in same st and in ea st across to next corner, * 2 sc in corner, sc in ea st across to next corner; rep from * around; join with sl st to beg sc.
Rnd 2: Ch 4 [counts as dc plus 1 ch], dc in same st, (ch 1, sk next st, dc in next st) across to corner, * (ch 1, dc) twice in corner, (ch 1, sk next st, dc in next st) across to next corner; rep from * around, ch 1; join with sl st to 3rd ch of beg ch-4.
Rnd 3: Ch 3, 2 dc in next ch-1 sp, dc in next dc, (dc in next ch-1 sp, dc in next dc) across to next corner, * 2 dc in corner ch-1 sp, (dc in next ch-1 sp, dc in next dc) across to next corner; rep from * around; join with sl st to top of beg ch-3.
Rnd 4: Ch 4, sk next dc, (dc, ch 1, dc) in next dc, (ch 1, sk next st, dc in next st) across to corner, * (ch 1, dc) twice in corner, (ch 1, sk next st, dc in next st) across to next corner; rep from * around, ch 1; join with sl st to 3rd ch of beg ch-4.
Rnd 5: Ch 1, sc in same st, sc in next ch-1 sp, * 7 dc in next ch-1 sp, sc in next ch-1 sp, sc in next dc, sc in next ch-1 sp; rep from * around; join with sl st to beg sc; fasten off.

Project was stitched with Jiffy: White #100.

Making Waves

Rock the boat with this innovative design. Just work from short stitches to tall ones and back for each wave.

Materials
Worsted-weight acrylic yarn, approximately:
24 oz. (1,250 yd.) royal blue, MC
18 oz. (940 yd.) light blue, A
18 oz. (940 yd.) cream, B
Size I crochet hook or size to obtain gauge

Finished Size
Approximately 53" x 62"

Gauge
In pat, 14 sts and 12 rows= 4"

Note: To change colors, work last yo of prev st with new color, dropping prev color to ws of work. Do not carry yarn across row.

With MC, ch 177, drop MC, pick up A, yo and pull through lp on hook [color change ch made]; with A, ch 2: 180 chs.

Row 1 (rs): With A, dc in 4th ch from hook, * hdc in next ch, sc in next ch, ch 2, sk next 2 chs, sc in next ch, hdc in next ch, dc in next 2 chs **, tr in next 2 chs, dc in next 2 chs; rep from * across, ending last rep at **: 178 sts.

Row 2: Ch 3 [counts as first dc], turn; sk first dc, dc in next dc, * hdc in next hdc, sc in next sc, ch 2, sk next 2 ch, sc in next sc, hdc in next hdc, dc in next 2 dc **, tr in next 2 tr, dc in next 2 dc; rep from * across, ending last rep at **, change to MC in last st.

Row 3: With MC, ch 1, turn; sc in first 4 sts, * working in front of next 2 chs on prev row, sc in next 2 foundation chs, sc in next 10 sts; rep from * across to last 4 sts, sc in last 4 sts.

Row 4: Ch 1, turn; sc in first sc and in ea sc across, change to B in last sc.

Row 5: With B, ch 1, turn; sc in first sc, * hdc in next sc, dc in next 2 dc, tr in next 2 sc, dc in next 2 sc, hdc in next sc, sc in next sc **, ch 2, sk next 2 sc, sc in next sc; rep from * across, ending last rep at **.

Row 6: Ch 1, turn; sc in first sc, * hdc in next hdc, dc in next 2 dc, tr in next 2 tr, dc in next 2 dc, hdc in next hdc, sc in next sc **, ch 2, sk next 2 chs, sc in next sc; rep from * across, ending last rep at **, change to MC in last st.

Row 7: With MC, ch 1, turn; sc in first 10 sts, * working in front of next 2 chs on prev row, sc in next 2 sk sts 2 rows below, sc in next 10 sc; rep from * across.

Row 8: Ch 1, turn; sc in first sc and in ea sc across, change to A in last sc.

Row 9: With A, ch 3, turn; sk first dc, dc in next sc, * hdc in next sc, sc in next sc, ch 2, sk next 2 sc, sc in next sc, hdc in next sc, dc in next 2 sc **, tr in next 2 sc, dc in next 2 sc; rep from * across, ending last rep at **.

Row 10: Rep row 2.

Row 11: With MC, ch 1, turn; sc in first 4 sts, * working in front of next 2 chs on prev row, sc in next 2 sk sts 2 rows below, sc in next 10 sts; rep from * across to last 4 sts, sc in last 4 sts.

Rows 12–171: Rep rows 4–11, 20 times; fasten off A and B; do not fasten off MC.

Border

Rnd 1 (rs): With rs facing, 3 sc in same st, sc evenly across to next corner, * 3 sc in corner, sc evenly across to next corner; rep from * around; join with sl st to beg sc.

Rnd 2: Ch 1, turn; sc in ea sc across to corner, * 3 sc in corner, sc in ea sc across to next corner; rep from * around; join with sl st to beg sc; fasten off.

Project was stitched with Keepsake Sayelle: Royal Blue #109, Robin Blue #107, and Cream #98.

Windowpanes

This heathery gray throw combines single crochet and long post stitches into tiny windowpanes. It's a cozy companion on a rainy day.

Materials

Worsted-weight wool-blend yarn, approximately:
12 oz. (790 yd.) dark gray, MC
18 oz. (1,185 yd.) light gray, A
21 oz. (1,380 yd.) tan, B
Size J crochet hook or size to obtain gauge

Finished Size

Approximately 39" x 56"

Gauge

14 sc and 18 rows = 4"

Pattern Stitches

Front Post Double tr (FPdtr): Yo 3 times, insert hook from front to back around post of st indicated, yo and pull up lp, (yo and pull through 2 lps) 4 times; sk st behind FPdtr.

Front Post Long st (FPLst): Yo 5 times, insert hook from front to back around post of st indicated, yo and pull up lp, (yo and pull through 2 lps) 6 times; sk st behind FPLst.

Note: To change colors, work last yo of prev st with new color, dropping old color to ws of work. Do not carry yarn across row.

With MC, ch 125.
Row 1 (rs): With MC, sc in 2nd ch from hook and in ea ch across: 124 sc.
Row 2: Ch 1, turn; sc in first sc and in ea sc across, change to A in last sc: 124 sc.
Row 3: With A, ch 1, turn; sc in first sc and in ea sc across.
Row 4: Ch 1, turn; sc in first sc and in ea sc across, change to B in last sc.
Rows 5–7: With B, ch 1, turn; sc in first sc and in ea sc across.
Row 8: Rep row 2.
Row 9: With A, ch 1, turn; sc in first sc and in next 2 sc, * (FPdtr around next st 5 rows below) twice, sc in next 4 sc, (FPdtr around next st 5 rows below) twice, sc in next 2 sc; rep from * across, ending with sc in last st.
Row 10: Ch 1, turn; sc in first sc and in ea sc across, change to MC in last sc.
Row 11: With MC, ch 1, turn; sc in first sc, * (FPLst around next st 9 rows below) twice, sc in next 8 sts; rep from * across to last 3 sts, (FPLst around next st 9 rows below) twice, sc in last st.

Rep rows 2–11 for pat until piece measures approximately 52" from beg, ending with row 2; do not fasten off.

Border

Rnds 1 and 2 (ws): With ws facing, ch 1, sc in same st; working in ends of rows, sc evenly across to corner, * 3 sc in corner, sc evenly across to next corner; rep from * around; join with sl st to beg sc; fasten off after last rnd.
Rnd 3: With ws facing, join B in top right corner with sl st, sc in same st, sc in ea st across to corner, * 3 sc in corner, sc in ea st across to next corner; rep from * around; join with sl st to beg sc.
Rnds 4–6: Ch 1, sc in same sc and in ea sc across to corner, * 3 sc in corner, sc in ea st across to corner; rep from * around; join with sl st to beg sc; fasten off after last row.
Rnd 7: With rs facing, join MC in bottom left corner with sl st; working from left to right, sc in same st and in ea st around [reverse sc]; join with sl st to beg sc; fasten off.

Project was stitched with Wool-Ease: Oxford Grey #152, Grey Heather #151, and Wheat #402.

Chenille Stripes

This soft afghan, with its rows of rich colors, makes a comfy chair even more inviting.

Materials
Worsted-weight chenille
  yarn, approximately:
8½ oz. (525 yd.) black, MC
7 oz. (435 yd.) brown, A
7 oz. (435 yd.) green, B
8½ oz. (525 yd.) maroon, C
Size H crochet hook or size to
  obtain gauge

Finished Size
Approximately 40" x 57"

Gauge
In pat, 10 dc and 8 rows = 4"

Note: To change colors, work last yo of prev st with new color, dropping prev color to ws of work. Do not carry yarn across row.

Pattern Stitch
Long dc (Ldc): Yo, insert hook in sp indicated, pull up ¾" lp, (yo and draw through 2 lps) twice.

With MC, ch 121.
Row 1 (rs): Dc in 4th ch from hook and in next ch, * ch 1, sk next ch, dc in next 3 chs; rep from * across: 90 dc.
Row 2: Ch 3 [counts as first dc throughout], turn; dc in next 2 dc, * ch 1, dc in next 3 dc; rep from * across, dc in top of tch, change to A in last st: 90 dc.
Row 3: With A, ch 4 [counts as first dc plus ch 1 throughout], turn; sk next dc, dc in next dc, * Ldc in ch-1 sp 2 rows below, dc in next dc, ch 1, sk next dc, dc in next dc; rep from * across.
Row 4: Ch 4, turn; * dc in next dc, dc in Ldc, dc in next dc, ch 1; rep from * across, dc in 3rd ch of beg ch-4, change to B in last st: 90 dc.
Row 5: With B, ch 3, turn; * Ldc in ch-1 sp 2 rows below, dc in next dc, ch 1, sk next dc, dc in next dc; rep from * across, Ldc in ch-1 sp 2 rows below, dc in 3rd ch of beg ch-4.
Row 6: Ch 3, turn; dc in Ldc, dc in next dc, * ch 1, dc in next dc, dc in Ldc, dc in next dc; rep from * across, change to C in last st: 90 dc.
Row 7: With C, ch 4, turn; sk next dc, dc in next dc, * Ldc in ch-1 sp 2 rows below, dc in next dc, ch 1, sk next dc, dc in next dc; rep from * across.
Row 8: Ch 4, turn; * dc in next dc, dc in Ldc, dc in next dc, ch 1; rep from * across, dc in 3rd ch of beg ch-4, change to MC in last st: 90 dc.
Row 9: With MC, ch 3, turn; * Ldc in ch-1 sp 2 rows below, dc in next dc, ch 1, sk next dc, dc in next dc; rep from * across, Ldc in ch-1 sp 2 rows below, dc in 3rd ch of beg ch-4.
Row 10: Rep row 2.

Rep rows 3–10 until afghan measures approximately 52" from beg ch, ending with row 10; do not change colors or fasten off.

Border
Rnd 1 (rs): Ch 1, turn; sc in ea st and ea ch-1 sp across to corner, * 3 sc in corner, sc evenly across to next corner; rep from * around; join with sl st to beg sc.
Rnd 2: Ch 3, turn; (sk 1 sc, sc in next sc, ch 1) across to corner, * (sc, ch 1) twice in corner sp, (sk 1 sc, sc in next sc, ch 1) across to next corner; rep from * around; join with sl st to beg ch; fasten off.
Rnd 3: With rs facing, join C with sl st in corner sp, ch 3, dc in same sp, (dc in next ch-1 sp, ch 1) across to next corner, * (2 dc, ch 1, 2 dc) in corner sp, (dc in next ch-1 sp, ch 1) across to next corner; rep from * around, 2 dc in corner sp, ch 1; join with sl st to top of beg ch-3; fasten off.
Rnd 4: With rs facing, join B with sl st in corner sp, ch 3, dc in same sp, ch 1, sk 2 dc, (sc in next dc, ch 1) across to last 2 dc, sk 2 dc, * (2 dc, ch 1, 2 dc) in corner sp, ch 1, sk 2 dc, (sc in next dc, ch 1) across to last 2 dc, sk 2 dc; rep from * around, 2 dc in corner sp, ch 1; join with sl st to top of beg ch-3; fasten off.
Rnd 5: With rs facing, join C with sl st in corner sp, ch 3, dc in same sp, ch 1, (dc in next ch-1 sp, ch 1) across to next corner, * (2 dc, ch 1, 2 dc) in corner sp, ch 1, (dc in next ch-1 sp, ch 1) across to next corner; rep from * around, 2 dc in corner sp, ch 1; join with sl st to top of beg ch-3.
Rnd 6: * Ch 3, sc in first ch of ch-3 just made [picot made], sc in next st, sl st in next st; rep from * around; join with sl st to base of first picot; fasten off.

Project was stitched with Chenille: Black #153, Brick #134, Forest Green #131, and Mulberry #142.

Diamond Filigree

Each block of this cool blue-and-white afghan contains a delicate diamond of lacy stitches.

Materials

- Worsted-weight wool-blend yarn, approximately:
- 36 oz. (2,370 yd.) blue-flecked white
- Size G crochet hook or size to obtain gauge
- Yarn needle

Finished Size

Approximately 43" x 58"

Gauge

Ea Square = 7½"

Square (Make 35.)

Center
Ch 10, join with sl st to form ring.
Rnd 1 (rs): Ch 3, 4 dc in ring, (ch 9, 5 dc in ring) 3 times, ch 9; join with sl st to top of beg ch-3.
Note: Mark last rnd as rs.
Rnd 2: Ch 3, dc in first dc, 2 dc in next dc, dc in next 2 dc, ch 2, (3 dc, ch 5, 3 dc) in next ch-9 sp, ch 2, * dc in next 2 dc, 2 dc in next dc, dc in next 2 dc, ch 2, (3 dc, ch 5, 3 dc) in next ch-9 sp, ch 2; rep from * around; join with sl st in top of beg ch-3.
Rnd 3: Ch 3, (yo, pull up lp in next dc, yo and pull through 2 lps) 5 times, yo and pull through all 6 lps on hook [beg cl made], * ch 6, sk next dc, dc in next dc, ch 3, (2 dc, ch 2, 2 dc) in next ch-5 sp, ch 3, sk next dc, dc in next dc, ch 5 **, sk next dc, (yo, pull up lp in next dc, yo and pull

through 2 lps) 6 times, yo and pull through all 7 lps on hook; rep from * around, ending last rep at **; join with sl st to beg cl.
Rnd 4: Ch 1, * 5 sc in next ch-6 sp, sc in next dc, 3 sc in next ch-3 sp, sc in next 2 dc, 2 sc in next ch-2 sp, sc in next 2 dc, 3 sc in next ch-3 sp, sc in next dc, 5 sc in next ch-5 sp; rep from * around; join with sl st to beg sc; fasten off.

Corner
Row 1: With ws facing, join yarn in any corner with sl st, ch 1, sc in first sc and in ea sc across to next corner: 24 sc.
Rows 2–12: Ch 1, turn; sk first sc, sc in ea sc across to last sc, sk last sc.
Row 13: Ch 1, turn; sk first sc, sl st in next sc; fasten off.
Rep for rem 3 corners.

Assembly

Afghan is 7 squares long and 5 squares wide. Whipstitch squares tog.

Border

With ws facing, attach yarn to corner with sl st, ch 1, sc in same st, sc evenly across to next corner, * 3 sc in corner, sc evenly across to next corner; rep from * around; join with sl st to beg sc; fasten off.

Edging

Note: Edging is worked sideways and attached to afghan as you go.

Ch 6, join with sl st to corner of afghan.
Row 1: (Dc, ch 2) twice in 5th ch of beg ch-6, (dc, ch 2, dc) in last ch.
Row 2: Ch 5, turn; sk first ch-2 sp, (dc, ch 2) 4 times in next ch-2 sp, join to Afghan with sl st so that Edging lies flat [approximately every 6th sc].
Row 3 (rs): Ch 2, turn; sk first ch-2 sp, (dc, ch 2) 3 times in next ch-2 sp, dc in same ch-2 sp.

Rep rows 2 and 3 across to corner, ending with row 2; * rep row 3, (rep rows 2 and 3) twice, joining with sl st in same corner; rep rows 2 and 3 across to next corner, ending with row 2; rep from * around, (rep row 3, rep row 2) twice in last corner; fasten off.

Sew first and last rows tog.
Note: Beg working in rnds.
Rnd 1: Join yarn in corner ch-5 sp with sl st, ch 3, 7 dc in same ch-5 sp, 8 dc in ea ch-5 sp around; join with sl st to top of beg ch-3; fasten off.

Project was stitched with Wool-Ease: Wedgewood Sprinkles #160.

Sampler Squares

Showcase your skill with four patterns in one afghan. Each block features a different stitch.

Materials

Worsted-weight wool yarn, approximately:
40 oz. (2,325 yd.) cream
Size H crochet hook or size to obtain gauge

Finished Size

Approximately 43" x 56"

Gauge

Ea Square = 9", without edging

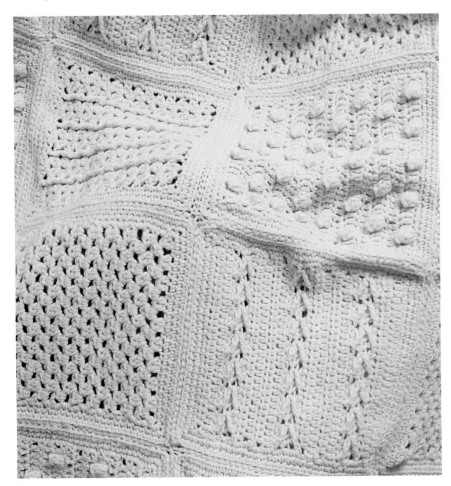

Popcorn Square (Make 5.)
Ch 31.
Row 1 (rs): Dc in 4th ch from hook, 5 dc in next ch, drop lp from hook, insert hook in first dc of 5-dc grp, pick up dropped lp and pull through [popcorn made], * dc in next 5 chs, popcorn in next ch; rep from * across to last 2 chs, dc in last 2 chs: 5 popcorns.
Note: Mark last row as rs.
Row 2: Ch 3 [counts as dc throughout], turn; sk first dc, dc in ea st across, dc in top of tch: 28 dc.
Row 3: Ch 3, turn; sk first dc, dc in next 4 dc, * popcorn in next dc, dc in next 5 dc, popcorn; rep from * across: 4 popcorns.
Row 4: Rep row 2.
Row 5: Ch 3, turn; sk first dc, dc in next dc, popcorn in next dc, * dc in next 5 dc, popcorn; rep from * across to last 2 dc, dc in last 2 dc.
Rows 6–15: Rep rows 2–5 twice, then rep rows 2 and 3 once; fasten off.

Popcorn Square Edging
Rnd 1 (rs): With rs facing, join yarn in top right corner with sl st, sc in same st and in ea st across to corner, 3 sc in corner, * sc evenly across to next corner, 3 sc in corner; rep from * around; join with sl st in beg sc.
Rnds 2 and 3: Ch 1, sc in ea sc across to corner, 3 sc in corner, * sc evenly across to next corner, 3 sc in corner; rep from * around; join with sl st in beg sc; fasten off after last rnd.

Shell Square (Make 5.)

Ch 34.
Row 1 (rs): (2 dc, ch 1, 2 dc) in 7th ch from hook [shell made], * sk 2 ch, dc in next ch, sk 2 ch, shell in next ch; rep from * across, dc in last ch: 5 shells.
Note: Mark last row as rs.
Row 2: Ch 3, turn; shell in first shell [ch-1 sp], * yo, insert hook from back to front around post of next dc, yo and pull up lp, (yo and pull through 2 lps) twice [BPdc

(continued)

Project was stitched with Fishermen's Wool: Natural #98.

made], shell in next shell; rep from * across, dc in 2nd ch of beg ch-6.

Row 3: Ch 3, turn; shell in first shell, * yo, insert hook from front to back around post of next dc, yo and pull up lp, (yo and pull through 2 lps) twice [FPdc made], shell in next shell; rep from * across, dc in top of beg ch-3.

Rows 4–14: Rep rows 2 and 3 alternately, 5 times, then rep row 2 once; do not fasten off.

Shell Square Edging

Rnd 1 (rs): Ch 1, turn; * sc evenly across to corner, 3 sc in corner; rep from * around; join with sl st to beg sc.

Rnds 2 and 3: Work as for Popcorn Square Edging.

Lattice Square (Make 5.)

Ch 32.

Row 1 (rs): Hdc in 3rd ch from hook, * ch 1, sk 1 ch, hdc in next 2 chs; rep from * across, ending with ch 1, hdc in last ch: 10 ch-1 sps.

Note: Mark last row as rs.

Row 2: Ch 3 [counts as hdc throughout], turn; * 2 hdc in next ch-1 sp, ch 1; rep from * across, hdc in tch: 11 ch-sps.

Row 3: Ch 3, turn; hdc in first ch-1 sp, ch 1, * 2 hdc in next ch-1 sp, ch 1; rep from * across, 2 hdc in last ch-3 sp.

Rows 4–20: Rep rows 2 and 3 alternately, 8 times, then rep row 2 once; do not fasten off.

Lattice Square Edging

Work as for Shell Square Edging.

Cable Square (Make 5.)

Ch 31.

Row 1 (rs): Hdc in 4th ch from hook and in ea ch across: 29 hdc.

Note: Mark last row as rs.

Row 2: Ch 3 [counts as hdc throughout], turn; sk first hdc, hdc in ea hdc across.

Row 3: Ch 3, turn; * sk first 3 hdc, tr in next hdc; working behind tr just made, dc in 3 sk sts; rep from * across, dc in last hdc.

Row 4: Ch 3, turn; * sk first 3 hdc, tr in next hdc; working in front of tr just made, dc in 3 sk

Lattice	Cable	Popcorn	Shell
Popcorn	Lattice	Shell	Cable
Shell	Cable	Popcorn	Lattice
Popcorn	Lattice	Cable	Shell
Shell	Cable	Lattice	Popcorn

Placement Diagram

sts; rep from * across, dc in last hdc.

Rows 5–8: Rep row 2, 4 times.

Rows 9–14: Rep rows 3–8.

Rows 15 and 16: Rep rows 3 and 4.

Rows 17 and 18: Rep row 2 twice; do not fasten off.

Cable Square Edging

Work as for Shell Square Edging.

Assembly

Referring to *Placement Diagram,* whipstitch squares tog.

Border

Rnd 1 (rs): With rs facing, join yarn in top right corner with sl st, * sc in same st and in ea st across to corner, 3 sc in corner; rep from * around; join with sl st to beg sc.

Rnd 2: Ch 3, * (hdc in next st, ch 1, sk 1 st) across to corner, (hdc, ch 1, hdc) in corner; rep from * around; join with sl st to beg ch-3.

Rnd 3: Ch 3, turn; hdc in first ch-1 sp, * 4 hdc in corner, 2 hdc in next ch-1 sp and in ea ch-1 sp across to corner; rep from * around; join with sl st to beg ch-3.

Rnd 4: Rep rnd 2.

Rnd 5: Ch 1, sc in first ch-1 sp and in ea ch-1 sp across to corner, * 3 sc in corner, sc in ea ch-1 sp across to corner; rep from * around; join with sl st to beg sc; fasten off.

Stripes for Baby

Choose either of these baby blankets—Shell Stripes, left, or Chevron Stripes, right—for a memorable shower gift. Directions for both of these afghans appear on the following two pages.

Shell Stripes

Stitched with two strands of yarn, the subtle color variations occur when you change only one strand of color at a time.

Materials
Sportweight yarn, approximately:
15¾ oz. (1,765 yd.) white, MC
8¾ oz. (980 yd.) blue, A
7 oz. (785 yd.) pink, B
Size J crochet hook or size to obtain gauge

Finished Size
Approximately 36" x 37", not including fringe

Gauge
In pat, 5½ shells and 10 rows = 4"

Note: Afghan is stitched holding 2 strands of yarn tog throughout. To change 1 color, work last yo of prev st with new color. Fasten off old color, leaving 8" tail.

With 2 strands MC, ch 155.
Row 1 (rs): 3 dc in 5th ch from hook [shell made], * sk 2 ch, shell in next ch; rep from * across to last 2 ch, sk 1 ch, dc in last ch; drop 1 strand MC, pick up 1 strand A: 51 shells.
Row 2: With 1 strand ea MC and A, ch 1, turn; sc in first dc, ch 1, sc in center dc of first shell, * ch 2, sc in center dc of next shell; rep from * across, ch 1, sc in top of beg ch-3.
Row 3: Ch 3, turn; sk first sc, shell in next sc and in ea sc across to last sc, dc in last sc, drop 1 strand MC, pick up 1 strand A.
Row 4: With 2 strands A, ch 1, turn; sc in first dc, ch 1, sc in center dc of first shell, * ch 2, sc in center dc of next shell; rep from * across, ch 1, sc in top of tch.
Row 5: Ch 3, turn; sk first sc, shell in next sc and in ea sc across to last sc, dc in last sc, drop 1 strand A, pick up 1 strand MC.
Row 6: Rep row 2.
Row 7: Rep row 5.
Row 8: With 2 strands MC, ch 1, turn; sc in first dc, ch 1, sc in center dc of first shell, * ch 2, sc in center dc of next shell; rep from * across, ch 1, sc in top of tch.
Row 9: Ch 3, turn; sk first sc, shell in next sc and in ea sc across to last sc, dc in last sc, drop 1 strand MC, pick up 1 strand B.
Row 10: With 1 strand ea MC and B, ch 1, turn; sc in first dc, ch 1, sc in center dc of first shell, * ch 2, sc in center dc of next shell; rep from * across, ch 1, sc in top of tch.
Row 11: Rep row 9.
Row 12: With 2 strands B, ch 1, turn; sc in first dc, ch 1, sc in center dc of first shell, * ch 2, sc in center dc of next shell; rep from * across, ch 1, sc in top of tch.
Row 13: Ch 3, turn; sk first sc, shell in next sc and in ea sc across to last sc, dc in last sc, drop 1 strand B, pick up 1 strand MC, ch 1, turn.
Row 14: Rep row 10.
Row 15: Rep row 13.
Row 16: Rep row 8.
Row 17: Rep row 3.
Rows 18–89: Rep rows 2–17, 4 times; then rep rows 2–9 once more, turn; do not fasten off.

Edging
Row 1: Sl st in first 2 dc, * ch 3, sl st in first ch of ch-3 just made [picot], sk next dc, sl st in next 2 dc; rep from * across, sl st in top of tch; fasten off, leaving 8" tail.
Row 2: With ws facing and working across bottom edge, attach 2 strands MC in corner with sl st, sl st in next ch, * picot, sk next ch, sl st in next 2 chs, rep from * across, sl st in last ch; fasten off, leaving 8" tail.

Fringe
For ea tassel, referring to page 143 of General Directions, cut 12 (11") lengths of yarn. Matching tassel color to row color, knot 1 tassel in end of every other row, securing 8" tail within tassel.

Project was stitched with Jamie Pompadour: White #200, Pastel Blue #206, and Pink #201.

Chevron Stripes

Work the same soft color changes as in Shell Stripes for a simple chevron pattern.

Materials
Sportweight yarn,
   approximately:
19¼ oz. (2,160 yd.) white, MC
8¾ oz. (980 yd.) aqua, A
7 oz. (785 yd.) lavender, B
Size I crochet hook or size to
   obtain gauge

Finished Size
Approximately 38½" x 44", not
including fringe

Gauge
In pat, 18 dc and 9 rows = 4"

Note: Afghan is stitched holding 2
strands of yarn tog throughout.
To change 1 color, work last yo of
prev st with new color. Fasten off
old color, leaving 8" tail.

With 2 strands MC, ch 202.
Row 1 (rs): Dc in 4th ch from
hook, (dc in next 3 chs, sk 2 chs,
dc in next 3 chs, 3 dc in next ch)
21 times, dc in next 3 chs, sk
2 chs, dc in next 3 chs, 2 dc in last
ch.
Row 2: Ch 1, turn; 2 sc in first dc,
(sc in next 3 dc, sk 2 dc, sc in next
3 dc, 3 sc in next dc) 21 times,
sc in next 3 dc, sk 2 dc, sc in next
3 dc, 2 sc in last dc, drop 1 strand
MC, pick up 1 strand A.
Row 3: With 1 strand ea MC and
A, ch 3, turn; working in bk lps
only, dc in first sc, (dc in next
3 sc, sk 2 sc, dc in next 3 sc, 3 dc
in next sc) 21 times, dc in next

3 sc, sk 2 sc, dc in next 3 sc, 2 dc
in last sc.
Row 4: Rep row 2.
Row 5: With 2 strands A, ch 3,
turn; working in bk lps only, dc in
first sc, (dc in next 3 sc, sk 2 sc,
dc in next 3 sc, 3 dc in next sc) 21
times, dc in next 3 sc, sk 2 sc,
dc in next 3 sc, 2 dc in last sc.
Row 6: Ch 1, turn; 2 sc in first dc,
(sc in next 3 dc, sk 2 dc, sc in next
3 dc, 3 sc in next dc) 21 times,
sc in next 3 dc, sk 2 dc, sc in next
3 dc, 2 sc in last dc, drop 1 strand
A, pick up 1 strand MC.
Row 7: Rep row 3.
Row 8: Rep row 6.
Row 9: With 2 strands MC, ch 3,
turn; working in bk lps only, dc in
first sc, (dc in next 3 sc, sk 2 sc,
dc in next 3 sc, 3 dc in next sc) 21
times, dc in next 3 sc, sk 2 sc,
dc in next 3 sc, 2 dc in last sc.
Row 10: Ch 1, turn; 2 sc in first
dc, (sc in next 3 dc, sk 2 dc, sc in
next 3 dc, 3 sc in next dc) 21
times, sc in next 3 dc, sk 2 dc,
sc in next 3 dc, 2 sc in last dc,
drop 1 strand MC, pick up 1
strand B.
Row 11: With 1 strand ea MC and
B, ch 3, turn; working in bk lps
only, dc in first sc, (dc in next 3 sc,
sk 2 sc, dc in next 3 sc, 3 dc in
next sc) 21 times, dc in next 3 sc,
sk 2 sc, dc in next 3 sc, 2 dc in last
sc.
Row 12: Rep row 10.
Row 13: With 2 strands B, ch 3,
turn; working in bk lps only, dc in
first sc, (dc in next 3 sc, sk 2 sc,
dc in next 3 sc, 3 dc in next sc) 21
times, dc in next 3 sc, sk 2 sc,

dc in next 3 sc, 2 dc in last sc.
Row 14: Ch 1, turn; 2 sc in first
dc, (sc in next 3 dc, sk 2 dc, sc in
next 3 dc, 3 sc in next dc) 21
times, sc in next 3 dc, sk 2 dc,
sc in next 3 dc, 2 sc in last dc,
drop 1 strand B, pick up 1 strand
MC, ch 3, turn.
Row 15: Rep row 11.
Row 16: Rep row 14.
   Cont in pat, working colors in
foll sequence: 2 rows ea MC, MC
and A tog, A, MC and A tog;
8 rows MC; 2 rows ea MC and B
tog, B, MC and B tog, MC, MC
and A tog, A, MC and A tog,
MC, MC and B tog, B, MC and B
tog; 8 rows MC; 2 rows ea MC
and A tog, A, MC and A tog,
MC, MC and B tog, B, MC and B
tog, MC, MC and A tog, A, MC
and A tog, MC.
   Do not fasten off after last row.

Edging
Row 1: Ch 1, turn; working in bk
lps only, sl st in ea st across; fasten
off, leaving 8" tail.
Row 2: With rs facing and working across bottom edge, join 2
strands MC with sl st in corner,
sl st in same ch and in ea ch
across; fasten off, leaving 8" tail.

Fringe
For ea tassel, referring to page
143 of General Directions, cut
12 (11") lengths of yarn. Matching
tassel color to row color, knot 1
tassel in end of every other row,
securing 8" tail within tassel.

Project was stitched with Jamie Pompadour: White #200, Aqua #271, and Lavender #244.

Hugs and Kisses

Alternate crossed stitches with clusters for rows and rows of Xs and Os. Add fringe to each side and then wrap it around someone you love.

Materials
Chunky-weight acrylic yarn, approximately:
72 oz. (2,220 yd.) burgundy
Size J crochet hook or size to obtain gauge

Finished Size
Approximately 48" x 60", without fringe

Gauge
In pat, 15 sts and 9 rows = 5"

Pattern Stitch
Cl: (Yo, insert hook in st indicated, yo and pull up lp, yo and pull through 2 lps on hook) 5 times, yo and draw through all 6 lps on hook.

Ch 144.
Row 1 (rs): Sc in 2nd ch from hook and in ea ch across: 143 sc.
Row 2: Ch 3 [counts as first dc throughout], turn; sk first 3 sc, tr in next sc, ch 1; working behind tr just made, tr in second sk sc, * ch 1, sk next sc, cl in next sc, ch 1, sk 3 sc, tr in next sc, ch 1; working behind tr just made, tr in second sk sc; rep from * across to last sc, dc in last sc: 23 cls.
Row 3: Ch 1, turn; sc in ea st and ch-1 sp across: 143 sc.
Row 4: Ch 4 [counts as first dc plus ch 1 throughout], turn; sk first 2 sc, cl in next sc, ch 1,

* sk 3 sc, tr in next sc, ch 1; working behind tr just made, tr in 2nd sk sc, ch 1, sk next sc, cl in next sc, ch 1; rep from * across to last sc, dc in last sc: 23 cls.
Row 5: Rep row 3.

Rep rows 2–5 until piece measures approximately 60", ending with an odd row; fasten off after last row.

Fringe
For ea tassel, referring to page 143 of General Directions, cut 1 (8") length of yarn. Working across short ends, knot 1 tassel in every st. Working across long ends, knot 1 tassel in end of ea sc row and 2 tassels in end of ea pat row.

Project was stitched with Homespun: Antique #307.

Pretty in Plaid

Turn a simple afghan of single crochet stripes into a stunning plaid blanket. Just slip stitch the vertical stripes on top of the finished afghan.

Materials
Worsted-weight wool-blend yarn, approximately:
18 oz. (1,185 yd.) green, MC
6 oz. (395 yd.) gray, A
6 oz. (395 yd.) blue, B
15 oz. (985 yd.) red, C
Size I crochet hook or size to obtain gauge

Finished Size
Approximately 49" x 55"

Gauge
14 sc and 17 rows = 4"

Note: To change colors, work last yo of prev st with new color, dropping prev color to ws of work.

With MC, ch 174.
Row 1: Sc in 2nd ch from hook and in next 12 chs, * ch 1, sk next ch, sc in next 2 chs, ch 1, sk next ch, (sc in next 5 chs, ch 1, sk next ch) twice, sc in next 2 chs, ch 1, sk next ch, sc in next 13 chs; rep from * across: 148 sc and 25 ch-1 sps.
Row 2: Ch 1, turn; sc in first 13 sc, * ch 1, sk next ch-1 sp, sc in next 2 sc, ch 1, sk next ch-1 sp, (sc in next 5 sc, ch 1, sk next ch-1 sp) twice, sc in next 2 sc, ch 1, sk next ch-1 sp, sc in next 13 sc; rep from * across.
Rows 3–6: Rep row 2, 4 times, changing to A in last st of last row.

Rows 7 and 8: With A, rep row 2 twice, changing to MC in last st of last row.
Rows 9–12: With MC, rep row 2, 4 times, changing to B in last st of last row.
Rows 13 and 14: With B, rep row 2 twice, changing to MC in last st of last row.
Rows 15–24: Rep rows 3–12 once; do not change colors.
Rows 25 and 26: With MC, rep row 2 twice, changing to C in last st of last row.
Rows 27–32: With C, rep row 2, 6 times, changing to B in last st of last row.
Rows 33 and 34: With B, rep row 2 twice, changing to C in last st of last row.
Rows 35–38: With C, rep row 2, 4 times, changing to A in last st of last row.
Rows 39 and 40: With A, rep row 2 twice, changing to C in last st of last row.
Rows 41–44: With C, rep row 2, 4 times, changing to B in last st of last row.

Rows 45–50: Rep rows 33–38 once; do not change colors after last row.
Rows 51 and 52: With C, rep row 2 twice, changing to MC in last st of last row.
Row 53: With MC, rep row 2 once.
Rows 54–234: Rep rows 2–53, 3 times, then rep rows 2–26 once; do not change colors; fasten off.

Stripes
With rs facing, join B in top right ch-1 sp with sl st, working vertically, sl st in ea ch-1 sp to bottom edge; fasten off.
Rep for ea vertical row of ch-1 sps, alternating B and A.

Border
With rs facing, join C in any corner with sl st, ch 1, 3 sc in same st, sc evenly across to next corner, * 3 sc in corner, sc evenly across to next corner; rep from * around; join with sl st to beg sc; fasten off.

Project was stitched with Wool-Ease: Green Heather #130, Slate Heather #108, Blue Mist #115, and Tapestry Heather #141.

Blue Basket Weave

Combine two yarns with different textures for variety. Be sure that the yarns are the same weight to keep the gauge accurate.

Materials
Chunky-weight brushed acrylic yarn, approximately: 24 oz. (1,080 yd.) light blue, MC
Chunky-weight acrylic yarn, approximately: 30 oz. (925 yd.) dark blue, CC
Size K crochet hook or size to obtain gauge

Finished Size
Approximately 48" x 60"

Gauge
In pat, 9 sts and 12 rows = 4"

Pattern Stitch
Long dc (Ldc): Yo, insert hook in sp indicated, pull up ¾" lp, (yo and draw through 2 lps) twice.

Note: To change colors, work last yo of prev st with new color, dropping prev color to ws of work. Do not carry yarn across row.

With MC, ch 105, drop MC, pick up CC, yo and pull through lp on hook [color change ch made]: 106 chs.
Row 1 (rs): With CC, sc in 2nd ch from hook and in ea ch across: 105 sc.
Row 2: Ch 1, turn; sc in first st and in ea st across, change to MC in last sc: 105 sc.
Row 3: With MC, ch 1, turn; sc in first 6 sc, * (sk next sc, Ldc in next st 3 rows below [foundation ch], sc in next sc) 5 times, sc in next 4 sc; rep from * across to last sc, sc in last sc.
Row 4: Ch 1, turn; sc in first st and in ea st across, change to CC in last sc: 105 sc.
Row 5: With CC, ch 1, turn; sc in first 7 sc, * (sk next sc, Ldc in next st 3 rows below, sc in next sc) 4 times, sc in next 6 sc; rep from * across.
Row 6: Rep row 2.
Row 7: With MC, ch 1, turn; sc in first 6 sc, * (sk next sc, Ldc in next st 3 rows below, sc in next sc) 5 times, sc in next 4 sc; rep from * across to last sc, sc in last sc.
Row 8: Rep row 4.
Row 9: With CC, ch 1, turn; sc in first sc, * (sk next sc, Ldc in next st 3 rows below, sc in next sc) 3 times **, sc in next 8 sc; rep from * across, ending last rep at **.
Row 10: Rep row 2.
Row 11: With MC, ch 1, turn; sc in first 2 sc, * (sk next sc, Ldc in next st 3 rows below, sc in next sc) twice **, sc in next 10 sc; rep from * across, ending last rep at **, sc in last sc.
Rows 12–14: Rep rows 8–10.
Rows 15–175: Rep rows 3–14, 13 times, then rep rows 3–7 once; fasten off MC, but do not fasten off CC.

Border
Rnd 1 (rs): With rs facing and CC, 2 sc in same st, work 127 sc evenly sp across ends of rows to next corner, 3 sc in corner, sc in ea ch across to next corner, 3 sc in corner, work 127 sc evenly sp across ends of rows to next corner, 2 sc in corner; join with sl st to beg sc of row 175.
Rnd 2 (ws): Ch 1, turn; sc in first sc and in ea sc across to next corner, * 3 sc in corner, sc in ea sc across to next corner; rep from * around; join with sl st to beg sc; fasten off.

Project was stitched with Jiffy, Dusty Blue #108; and Homespun, Colonial #302.

Double Delight

Work this sturdy afghan by holding two strands together as you stitch. You'll appreciate the extra warmth during a cold winter.

Materials
Worsted-weight wool-blend yarn, approximately: 78 oz. (5,125 yd.) natural
Size N crochet hook or size to obtain gauge

Finished Size
Approximately 52" x 63"

Gauge
In pat, 8 sts and 10 rows = 4"

Pattern Stitches
Puff: (Yo, insert hook in st indicated, yo and pull up lp) 3 times, yo and pull through all 7 lps on hook.
Front Post dc (FPdc): Yo, insert hook from front to back around post of st indicated, yo and pull up lp, (yo and pull through 2 lps) twice; sk st behind FPdc.

Note: Afghan is worked holding 2 strands of yarn tog throughout.

Ch 104.
Row 1 (rs): Sc in 2nd ch from hook and in ea ch across: 103 sc.
Row 2: Ch 1, turn; sc in first 7 sc, (puff in next sc, sc in next 10 sc) across to last 8 sc, puff in next sc, sc in last 7 sc: 9 puffs.
Row 3: Ch 1, turn; sc in first sc, * FPdc around next 2 sc on row 1, sc in next 3 sc, FPdc around next sc on row 1, sc in top of puff, FPdc around next sc on row 1, sc in next 3 sc; rep from * across to last 3 sc, FPdc around next 2 sc on row 1, sc in last sc.
Row 4: Ch 1, turn; sc in first sc and in ea st across: 103 sc.
Row 5: Ch 1, turn; sc in first sc, * FPdc around next 2 FPdc, sc in next 3 sc, sk next FPdc and sc, FPdc around next FPdc; working behind last st, sc in sk sc; working in front of last FPdc, FPdc around sk FPdc, sc in next 3 sc; rep from * across to last 3 sts, FPdc around next 2 FPdc, sc in last sc.
Row 6: Rep row 2.
Row 7: Ch 1, turn; sc in first sc, * FPdc around next 2 FPdc, sc in next 3 sc, FPdc around next FPdc, sc in top of puff, FPdc around next FPdc, sc in next 3 sc; rep from * across to last 3 sc, FPdc around next 2 FPdc, sc in last sc.
Rows 8 and 9: Rep rows 4 and 5.
Rows 10–157: Rep rows 6–9, 37 times; fasten off after last row.

Border
With rs facing, join yarn in any corner with sl st, ch 1, sc in same st, sc evenly across to next corner, * 3 sc in corner, sc evenly across to next corner; rep from * around; join with sl st to beg sc; fasten off.

To keep the puffs from flattening, tack the crossed post stitches down in the center, using two strands of yarn and a yarn needle.

Project was stitched with Wool-Ease: Wheat #402.

Loop-a-Minute

Create strips of color quickly with this easy technique. Simply twist the chains before you work into them to create the loops.

Materials

Chunky-weight brushed acrylic yarn, approximately:

Large Afghan: 18 oz. (810 yd.) blue, MC
15 oz. (675 yd.) rose, A
15 oz. (675 yd.) green, B
15 oz. (675 yd.) cream, C

Small Afghan: 9 oz. (405 yd.) light blue, MC
6 oz. (270 yd.) pink, A
6 oz. (270 yd.) light green, B
6 oz. (270 yd.) yellow, C
Size J crochet hook or size to obtain gauge

Finished Sizes

Large Afghan: Approximately 55¼" x 63", without tassels
Small Afghan: Approximately 38½" x 38½", without tassels

Gauge

11 sc = 4"
Ea Strip = 4¼" wide

Note: Directions are written for Large Afghan, with Small Afghan in braces.

Strip (Make 4 with MC and 3 ea with A, B, and C.) {Make 3 with MC and 2 ea with A, B, and C.} Ch 166 {100}.
Row 1 (rs): Sc in 2nd ch from hook and in ea ch across: 165 {99} sc.
Note: Mark last row as rs.

Row 2: Ch 4 [counts as first dc plus 1 ch throughout], turn; sk first 2 sc, (dc in next sc, ch 1, sk 1 sc) across to last sc, dc in last sc.
Row 3: Ch 1, turn; sc in ea dc and ch-1 sp across: 165 {99} sc.
Note: Beg working in rnds.
Rnd 1 (rs): (Ch 8, sl st around beg ch-4 of row 2) twice, ch 8, sl st in free lp of beg ch, mark 3 ch-8 lps just made; (ch 8, sk 1 ch, sl st into free lp of next ch) across beg ch; (ch 8, sl st around last dc of row 2) twice, ch 8, sl st in first sc of row 3, mark 3 ch-8 lps just made; (ch 8, sk 1 sc, sl st into next sc) across: 170 {104} ch-8 lps.
Rnd 2 (rs): Twisting first ch-8 lp counterclockwise, sl st in last 2 chs of ch-8 lp, ch 3 [counts as first dc], 3 dc in top of same ch-8 lp; (twisting next ch-8 lp counter-clockwise, 4 dc in top of ch-8 lp)

twice; (twisting next ch-8 lp counterclockwise, 3 dc in top of next ch-8 lp) across to next marked ch-8 lp; (twisting next ch-8 lp counterclockwise, 4 dc in top of ch-8 lp) 3 times; (twisting next ch-8 lp counterclockwise, 3 dc in top of next ch-8 lp) across to next beg ch-8 lp; join with sl st to top of beg ch-3; fasten off.

Assembly

Join 1 MC strip to 1 A strip as folls: with rs tog, MC, working in bk lps only, and beg at first 3-dc grp, sl st in ea st across to last 3-dc grp; fasten off.

Using color of prev Strip, cont joining strips in same manner in foll sequence: (A, B, C, MC) 3 times {twice}.

Tassels

For ea tassel, referring to page 143 of General Directions, wind yarn around 4" {3"} piece of cardboard 18 {15} times. Join 1 tassel to ea end of ea Strip.

Follow the directions within the braces to make a matching baby afghan.

Small Afghan was stitched with Jiffy: Pastel Blue #105, Melon #184, Mint #156, and Pastel Yellow #157.
Large Afghan was stitched with Jiffy: Heather Blue #111, Dusty Rose #141, Country Green #181, and Fisherman #99.

Touchable Texture

Worked in a soft chenille yarn, this snuggly afghan feels luxurious.
Long double crochet stitches create an allover raised pattern.

Materials

Worsted-weight chenille yarn,
approximately:
50½ oz. (3,135 yd.) burgundy
Sizes G and H crochet hooks or
sizes to obtain gauge

Finished Size

Approximately 49½" x 54½"

Gauge

In pat with larger hook, 12 sts and
12 rows = 4"

Pattern Stitch

Long dc (Ldc): Yo, insert hook in
st indicated, pull up ¾" lp, (yo and
draw through 2 lps) twice; sk st
behind Ldc.

With larger hook, ch 142.
Row 1 (rs): Sc in 2nd ch from
hook and in ea ch across: 141 sc.
Row 2: Ch 1, turn; sc in first sc
and in ea st across: 141 sc.
Row 3: Ch 1, turn; sc in first sc,
(Ldc in next sc 2 rows below, sc in
next sc) across.
Row 4: Rep row 2.
Row 5: Ch 1, turn; sc in first 2 sc,
(Ldc in next sc 2 rows below, sc in
next sc) across to last sc, sc in last
sc.

Rep rows 2–5 until piece measures approximately 52" from
beg; fasten off.

Border

Rnd 1 (rs): With rs facing and
smaller hook, join yarn to top
right corner with sl st, ch 1, 3 sc in
same st, sc in ea st across to corner, * 3 sc in corner, sc evenly
across to next corner; rep from *
around; join with sl st to beg sc.
Rnd 2: Sl st in bk lp only of corner
sc, ch 4; working in bk lps only,
(dc, ch 1, dc) in same st, (ch 1,
sk next sc, dc in next sc) across to
next corner, ch 1, * (dc, ch 1) 3
times in corner, (ch 1, sk next sc,
dc in next sc) across to next corner, ch 1; rep from * around; join
with sl st to 3rd ch of beg ch-4.
Rnd 3: Ch 1; working in both lps,
sc in same st and in next ch-1 sp,
* 3 sc in corner, sc in ea ch-1 sp
and ea dc across to next corner;
rep from * around; join with sl st
to beg sc.
Rnd 4 (ws): Turn; (ch 2, sl st in
2nd ch from hook, sk next sc, sl st
in ft lps only of next 3 sc) around;
join with sl st to beg sl st; fasten
off.

Project was stitched with Chenille Sensations: Mulberry #142.

Cape Cod

Stitch a seaside sampler in ocean blue and creamy white. Easy color changes in single crochet make up each patterned block.

Materials
Worsted-weight wool-blend yarn, approximately:
21 oz. (1,380 yd.) cream, MC
18 oz. (1,185 yd.) blue, CC
Size J crochet hook or size to obtain gauge

Finished Size
Approximately 46" x 54"

Gauge
14 sc and 16 rows = 4"
Ea Block = 7" without edging

Note: To change colors, work last yo of prev st with new color, dropping prev color to ws of work. Do not carry yarn across row.

Block A (Make 8.)
With CC, ch 25.
Row 1 (rs): Sc in 2nd ch from hook and in ea ch across: 24 sc.
Note: Mark last row as rs.
Row 2: Ch 1, turn; sc in first sc and in ea sc across: 24 sc.
Rep row 2, 26 times; do not fasten off.

Block A Edging
Rnd 1: Ch 1, turn; sc in first sc and in ea sc across to corner, * 3 sc in corner, sc evenly across to next corner; rep from * around; join with sl st to beg sc; fasten off.
Rnd 2: With rs facing, join MC in corner with sl st, sc in first sc and in ea sc across to corner, * 3 sc in corner, sc in ea sc across to corner; rep from * around; join with sl st to beg sc.
Rnds 3 and 4: Ch 1, sc in first sc and in ea sc across to corner, * 3 sc in corner, sc in ea sc across to corner; rep from * around; join with sl st to beg sc; fasten off after last rnd.

Block B (Make 8.)
With MC, ch 25.
Work as for Block A in foll color sequence: (1 row MC, 2 rows CC, 1 row MC, 4 rows CC) 3 times, 1 row MC, 2 rows CC, 1 row MC; fasten off after last row.

Block B Edging
Rnd 1: With rs facing, join CC in corner with sl st, ch 1, sc in first sc and in ea sc across to corner, * 3 sc in corner, sc evenly across to next corner; rep from * around; join with sl st to beg sc; fasten off.

(continued)

Project was stitched with Wool-Ease: Fisherman #99 and Blue Heather #107.

Rnds 2–4: Work as for Block A edging.

Block C (Make 7.)

With CC, ch 25.

Row 1 (ws): Sc in 2nd ch from hook and in next 3 chs, drop CC in front of work, change to MC in last st, sc in next 4 chs, * drop MC in front of work, change to CC in last st, sc in next 4 chs, drop CC in front of work, change to MC in last st, sc in next 4 chs; rep from * across: 24 sc.

Row 2 (rs): Ch 1, turn; sc in first 4 sc, drop MC in back of work, change to CC, sc in next 4 sc, * drop CC in back of work, change to MC, sc in next 4 sc, drop MC in back of work, change to CC, sc in next 4 sc; rep from * across.

Note: Mark last row as rs.

Row 3: Ch 1, turn; sc in first 4 sc, drop CC in front of work, change to MC, sc in next 4 sc, * drop MC in front of work, change to CC, sc in next 4 sc, drop CC in front of work, change to MC, sc in next 4 sc; rep from * across.

Row 4: Ch 1, turn; sc in first 4 sc, drop MC in back of work, change to CC, sc in next 4 sc, * drop CC in back of work, change to MC, sc in next 4 sc, drop MC in back of work, change to CC, sc in next 4 sc; rep from * across, change to MC in last st.

Rows 5 and 6: Rep rows 2 and 3.

Row 7: Rep row 2.

Row 8: Ch 1, turn; sc in first 4 sc, drop CC in front of work, change to MC, sc in next 4 sc, * drop MC in front of work, change to CC, sc in next 4 sc, drop CC in front of work, change to MC, sc in next 4 sc; rep from * across, change to CC in last st.

Row 9: Rep row 3.

Rows 10–27: Rep rows 2–9, twice, then rep rows 2 and 3 once.

Row 28: Rep row 2; fasten off.

Block C Edging
Work as for Block B Edging.

Block D (Make 7.)

With CC, ch 25.

Row 1 (rs): Sc in 2nd ch from hook and in ea ch across, change to MC in last st: 24 sc.

Note: Mark last row as rs.

Row 2: Ch 1, turn; sc in first sc, change to CC, sc in next sc, (change to MC, sc in next 4 sc, change to CC, sc in next sc, change to MC, sc in next 2 sc, change to CC, sc in next sc) twice, change to MC, sc in next 4 sc, change to CC, sc in next sc, change to MC, sc in last sc.

Row 3: Ch 1, turn; sc in first sc, change to CC, sc in next sc, (change to MC, sc in next 4 sc, change to CC, sc in next sc, change to MC, sc in next 2 sc, change to CC, sc in next sc) twice, change to MC, sc in next 4 sc, change to CC, sc in next sc, change to MC, sc in last sc, change to CC.

Row 4: Ch 1, turn; sc in first sc and in ea sc across, change to MC in last st.

Rows 5–7: Rep row 2.

Rows 8 and 9: Rep rows 3 and 4.

Rows 10–28: Rep rows 2–9 twice, then rep rows 2–4 once; do not change colors or fasten off.

Block D Edging
Work as for Block A Edging.

Assembly

Referring to *Assembly Diagram,* whipstitch Blocks tog with rs tog and using MC.

Border

Rnd 1 (rs): With rs facing, join MC in top right corner with sl st, sc in first sc and in ea sc across to corner, * 3 sc in corner, sc in ea sc across to corner; rep from * around; join with sl st to beg sc.

Rnd 2: Ch 1, sc in first sc and in ea sc across to corner, * 3 sc in corner, sc in ea sc across to corner; rep from * around; join with sl st to beg sc.

Rnd 3: Ch 4 [counts as dc plus ch], dc in same st, (ch 1, sk next sc, dc in next sc) across to corner, * (ch 1, dc) twice in corner, (ch 1, sk next sc, dc in next sc) across to corner; rep from * around, ch 1, dc in corner; join with sl st to 3rd ch of beg ch-4.

Rnd 4: Ch 4, dc in same st, (ch 1, dc in next dc) across to corner, * (ch 1, dc) twice in corner, (ch 1, sk next sc, dc in next sc) across to corner; rep from * around, ch 1, dc in corner; join with sl st to 3rd ch of beg ch-4.

Rnd 5: Ch 1, sc in ea dc and ea ch-1 sp across to corner, * 3 sc in corner, sc in ea dc and ea ch-1 sp across to corner; rep from * around, 2 sc in corner; join with sl st to beg sc.

Rnd 6: Ch 1, sc in ea sc across to corner, * 3 sc in corner, sc in ea sc across to corner; rep from * around, 2 sc in corner; join with sl st to beg sc; fasten off.

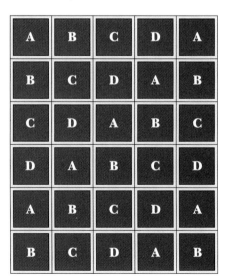

Assembly Diagram

Rustic Duo

Bold red and black stripes or checks add cheer to rustic decor.
Directions for both of these afghans appear on the following two pages.

Woodsman Stripes

Worked with two strands of yarn, this sturdy afghan will warm you up after a brisk woodland walk.

Materials
Chunky-weight brushed
  acrylic yarn, approximately:
45 oz. (2,025 yd.) black, MC
39 oz. (1,755 yd.) red, CC
Size N crochet hook or size to
  obtain gauge
Yarn needle

Finished Size
Approximately 54" x 64", without
fringe

Gauge
In pat, 7 sts and 6 rows = 4"

Note: Afghan is stitched holding
2 strands of yarn tog throughout.
To change 1 color, work last yo of
prev st with new color; fasten off
old color.

With 1 strand ea MC and CC tog,
ch 95.
Row 1 (rs): Sc in 2nd ch from
hook, dc in next ch, (sc in next ch,
dc in next ch) across: 94 sts.
Rows 2 and 3: Ch 1, turn; sc in
first dc, dc in next sc, (sc in next
dc, dc in next sc) across.
Row 4: Ch 1, turn; sc in first dc,
dc in next sc, (sc in next dc, dc in
next sc) across, drop CC, pick up
1 strand MC.
Rows 5–7: With 2 strands MC,
ch 1, turn; sc in first st and in ea st
across: 94 sc.
Row 8: Ch 1, turn; sc in first sc
and in ea sc across, drop 1 strand
MC, pick up 1 strand CC.

Row 9: With 1 strand ea of MC
and CC, rep row 2.
Row 10: Ch 1, turn; sc in first dc,
dc in next sc, (sc in next dc, dc in
next sc) across, drop MC, pick up
1 strand CC.
Rows 11–13: With 2 strands CC,
ch 1, turn; sc in first st and in ea st
across: 94 sc.
Row 14: Ch 1, turn; sc in first sc
and in ea sc across, drop 1 strand
CC, pick up 1 strand MC.
Row 15: With 1 strand ea of MC
and CC, rep row 2.

Rows 16–21: Rep rows 4–9.
   Rep row 2 until afghan measures approximately 43" from
beg; then rep rows 4–21 once;
then rep row 2, 4 times; fasten
off.

Fringe
For ea tassel, referring to page
143 of General Directions, cut 1
(6") length ea of MC and CC.
Working across short ends, knot 1
tassel in every st.

Project was stitched with Jiffy: Black #153 and Red #112.

Buffalo Checks

Whipstitch super-quick granny squares together to form this classic pattern.

Materials
Chunky-weight brushed
   acrylic yarn, approximately:
36 oz. (1,620 yd.) black, MC
36 oz. (1,620 yd.) red, CC
Size N crochet hook or size to
   obtain gauge
Yarn needle

Finished Size
Approximately 49½" x 58½"

Gauge
Ea Square = 4½"

Note: Afghan is stitched holding
2 strands of yarn tog throughout.

Black Square (Make 36.)
With 2 strands of MC, ch 3, join
with sl st to form ring.
Rnd 1 (rs): Ch 3 [counts as dc
throughout], 2 dc in ring, (ch 3,
3 dc in ring) 3 times, ch 3; join
with sl st to top of beg ch-3: 12 dc.
Note: Mark last rnd as rs.
Rnd 2: Sl st in next 2 dc, ch 3,
(2 dc, ch 3, 3 dc) in next ch-3 sp,
* (3 dc, ch 3, 3 dc) in next ch-3 sp;
rep from * around; join with sl st
to top of beg ch-3; fasten off.

Red Square (Make 35.)
Work as for Black Square, holding
2 strands of CC tog.

Red-and-Black Square
(Make 72.)
Work as for Black Square, holding
1 strand ea of MC and CC tog.

Project was stitched with Jiffy: Black #153 and Red #112.

Assembly
Referring to *Assembly Diagram,*
whipstitch squares tog.

Key

█ *2 strands red*

█ *2 strands black*

█ *1 strand ea red and black*

Assembly Diagram

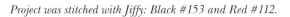

Playful Primaries

I like to bring a bright blanket outdoors and spend time reading with Nicholas. The cheerful colors of this afghan suit these happy times.

Materials

Worsted-weight yarn,
approximately:
12 oz. (600 yd.) blue, MC
12 oz. (600 yd.) red, A
12 oz. (600 yd.) yellow, B
12 oz. (600 yd.) green, C
Size J crochet hook or size to
obtain gauge

Finished Size

Approximately 40½" x 56"

Gauge

12 sts and 14 rows = 4"
Ea Block = 6¼"

Note: To change colors, work last yo of prev st with new color, dropping prev color to ws of work. Do not carry yarn across row.

Block 1 (Make 12.)

With MC, ch 8, drop MC, pick up A, yo and pull through lp on hook [color change ch made], with A, ch 12: 21 chs.
Row 1 (rs): With A, sc in 2nd ch from hook, sc in next 11 chs, change to MC, sc in ea ch across: 20 sc.
Note: Mark last row as rs.
Row 2: Ch 1, turn; sc in first 8 sc, change to A, sc in next 12 sc: 20 sc.
Row 3: Ch 1, turn; sc in first 12 sc, change to MC, sc in next 8 sc.
Rows 4–6: Rep rows 2 and 3 once, then rep row 2 once more.
Row 7: Ch 1, turn; sc in first 11 sc, change to MC, sc in next 9 sc.
Row 8: Ch 1, turn; sc in first 9 sc, change to A, sc in next 11 sc.
Row 9: Ch 1, turn; sc in first 10 sc, change to MC, sc in next 10 sc.
Row 10: Ch 1, turn; sc in first 10 sc, change to A, sc in next 10 sc.
Row 11: Rep row 9.
Row 12: Ch 1, turn; sc in first 11 sc, change to A, sc in next 9 sc.
Row 13: Ch 1, turn; sc in first 9 sc, change to MC, sc in next 11 sc.
Row 14: Ch 1, turn; sc in first 12 sc, change to A, sc in next 8 sc.
Row 15: Ch 1, turn; sc in first 7 sc, change to MC, sc in next 13 sc.
Row 16: Ch 1, turn; sc in first 14 sc, change to A, sc in next 6 sc.
Row 17: Ch 1, turn; sc in first 4 sc, change to MC, sc in next 16 sc.
Rows 18–22: Ch 1, turn; sc in first sc and in ea across; fasten off after last row.

Block 2 (Make 12.)

Work as for Block 1, reversing colors.

(continued)

Project was stitched with Jamie 4 Ply: Blue #109, Red #113, Buttercup #158, and Evergreen #130.

Block 3 (Make 12.)

With C, ch 12, drop C, pick up B, yo and pull through lp on hook [color change ch made], with B, ch 8: 21 chs.

Row 1 (rs): With B, sc in 2nd ch from hook, sc in next 7 chs, change to C, sc in ea ch across: 20 sc.

Note: Mark last rows as rs.

Row 2: Ch 1, turn; sc in first 12 sc, change to B, sc in next 8 sc.

Row 3: Ch 1, turn; sc in first 8 sc, change to C, sc in next 12 sc.

Rows 4–6: Rep rows 2 and 3 once, then rep row 2 once more.

Row 7: Ch 1, turn; sc in first 9 sc, change to C, sc in next 11 sc.

Row 8: Ch 1, turn; sc in first 11 sc, change to B, sc in next 9 sc.

Row 9: Ch 1, turn; sc in first 10 sc, change to C, sc in next 10 sc.

Row 10: Ch 1, turn; sc in first 10 sc, change to B, sc in next 10 sc.

Row 11: Rep row 9.

Row 12: Ch 1, turn; sc in first 9 sc, change to B, sc in next 11 sc.

Row 13: Ch 1, turn; sc in first 11 sc, change to C, sc in next 9 sc.

Row 14: Ch 1, turn; sc in first 8 sc, change to B, sc in next 12 sc.

Row 15: Ch 1, turn; sc in first 13 sc, change to C, sc in next 7 sc.

Row 16: Ch 1, turn; sc in first 6 sc, change to B, sc in next 14 sc.

Row 17: Ch 1, turn; sc in first 16 sc, change to C, sc in next 4 sc.

Rows 18–22: Ch 1, turn; sc in first sc and in ea sc across; fasten off after last row.

Block 4 (Make 12.)

Work as for Block 3, reversing colors.

Assembly

Referring to *Assembly Diagram,* whipstitch blocks tog.

Border

Rnd 1 (rs): With rs facing, join MC with sl st in top right corner, sc in same st, sc evenly across to corner, * 3 sc in corner, sc evenly across to next corner; rep from * around, sc in beg corner; join with sl st to beg sc.

Rnds 2–6: Sc in same st and in ea sc across to corner, * 3 sc in corner, sc in ea st across to corner; rep from * around, sc in beg corner; join with sl st to beg sc; fasten off after last rnd.

Assembly Diagram

Place Mats

Cotton yarn is a pretty and practical choice for these table settings. Match the colors to your favorite china or create country style with red-and-white or blue-and-white checks.

Materials (for 2 place mats)
Worsted-weight cotton yarn, approximately:
5 oz. (235 yd.) navy, MC
5 oz. (235 yd.) green, A
5 oz. (235 yd.) rose, B
Size H crochet hook or size to obtain gauge

Finished Size
Approximately 11½" x 16", without fringe

Gauge
14 sc and 14 rows = 4"

Note: To change colors, work last yo of prev st with new color, dropping prev color to ws of work. Carry yarn not in use loosely across row.

With MC, ch 57.
Row 1 (rs): Sc in 2nd ch from hook and in next 7 chs, * change to A, sc in next 8 chs, change to MC, sc in next 8 chs; rep from * across: 56 sc.
Rows 2–8: Ch 1, turn; with MC, sc in first 8 sc, * change to A, sc in next 8 sc, change to MC, sc in next 8 sc; rep from * across, changing to B in last st of last row.
Rows 9–16: Ch 1, turn; with B, sc in first 8 sc, * change to MC, sc in next 8 sc, change to B, sc in next 8 sc; rep from * across, changing to MC in last st of last row.
Row 17: Rep row 2 once.
Rows 18–40: Rep rows 2–17 once, then rep rows 2–8 once; fasten off after last row.

Fringe
For ea tassel, referring to page 143 of General Directions, cut 3 (8") lengths of MC or B. Working across short ends and matching colors, knot 1 tassel in approximately every 3rd st.

Project was stitched with Kitchen Cotton: Navy #110, Forest Green #131, and Rose #140.

Wheels of Popcorn

Surround pink and purple circles with soft, variegated yarn.
A pink puff-stitch border and extralong fringe make this
afghan a sure winner.

Materials
Chunky-weight brushed
  acrylic yarn, approximately:
18 oz. (810 yd.) rose, MC
12 oz. (540 yd.) lavender, A
20 oz. (920 yd.) rose-and-
  lavender variegated, B
Size J crochet hook or size to
  obtain gauge
Yarn needle

Finished Size
Approximately 43" x 59", without
fringe

Gauge
Ea Square = 8"

Pattern Stitches
Popcorn: 4 dc in st indicated,
drop lp from hook, insert hook in
first dc of 4-dc grp, pull dropped
lp through.
Puff: (Yo, insert hook in sp indicated, yo and pull up lp) 4 times,
yo and pull through all 9 lps on
hook, ch 1 to close.

Square 1 (Make 17.)
With MC, ch 6, join with sl st to
form ring.
Rnd 1 (rs): Ch 5 [counts as tr plus
ch], (tr in ring, ch 1) 15 times; join
with sl st to 4th ch of beg ch-5: 16
ch-1 sps.
Note: Mark last rnd as rs.
Rnd 2: Ch 4, 3 dc in first ch-1 sp,
drop lp from hook, insert hook in
4th ch of beg ch-4, pull dropped
lp through [beg popcorn made],
ch 2, (popcorn in next ch-1 sp,
ch 2) 15 times; join with sl st to
top of beg ch-4; fasten off.
Rnd 3: Join B in any ch-2 sp with
sl st, (ch 3, 3 dc, ch 2, 4 dc) in
same sp as joining [corner made],
ch 3, * (sc in next ch-2 sp, ch 3) 3
times, (4 dc, ch 2, 4 dc) in next
ch-2 sp; rep from * twice, ch 3,
(sc in next ch-2 sp, ch 3) 3 times;
join with sl st to top of beg ch-3.
Rnd 4: Sl st in next 3 dc, sl st in
next ch-2 sp, ch 3, (3 dc, ch 2, 4 dc)
in same ch-2 sp, * ch 1, sk next
ch-3 sp, (4 dc in next ch-3 sp,
ch 1) twice, sk next ch-3 sp, (4 dc,
ch 2, 4 dc) in corner ch-2 sp; rep
from * twice, ch 1, sk next ch-3 sp,
(4 dc in next ch-3 sp, ch 1) twice;
join with sl st to top of beg ch-3;
fasten off.
Rnd 5: Join A in corner ch-2 sp
with sl st, ch 3, (3 dc, ch 2, 4 dc)
in same sp as joining, * (4 dc in
next ch-1 sp) 3 times, (4 dc, ch 2,
4 dc) in next corner ch-2 sp; rep
from * twice, (4 dc in next
ch-1 sp) 3 times; join with sl st to
top of beg ch-3; fasten off.

Square 2 (Make 18.)
Work as for Square 1, reversing
MC and A.

Assembly
Afghan is 5 squares wide and 7
squares long. Whipstitch squares
tog in checkerboard pattern.

Border
Rnd 1 (rs): With rs facing, join
MC in any corner with sl st, ch 1,
* (sc, ch 2, sc) in same sp as joining, sc in ea st across to next corner; rep from * around; join with
sl st to beg sc.
Rnd 2: Sl st in corner ch-2 sp,
* (puff, ch 2, puff) in same corner
ch-2 sp, (ch 1, sk next sc, puff in
next sc) across to next corner
ch-2 sp; rep from * around, ch 1;
join with sl st to top of beg puff.
Rnd 3: Sl st in corner ch-2 sp, ch 3,
sc in same sp, * sc in top of ea puff
and ea ch-1 sp across to corner,
(sc, ch 2, sc) in corner ch-2 sp; rep
from * around; join with sl st to
beg sc.
Rnd 4: Sl st in corner ch-2 sp,
ch 3, sc in same sp, * sc in ea sc
across to corner, (sc, ch 2, sc) in
corner ch-2 sp; rep from *
around; join with sl st to beg sc;
fasten off.

Fringe
For ea tassel, referring to page
143 of General Directions, cut 5
(16") lengths of B. Working across
short ends, knot 1 tassel in every
3rd st.

Project was stitched with Jiffy: Rose #140, Lilac #144, and Salem #330.

Zigzag Zebra

Make a dramatic statement with strong stripes. Frosted yarn and puff stitches jazz up this classic ripple design.

Materials

Worsted-weight wool-blend
 yarn, approximately:
15 oz. (975 yd.) black, MC
25 oz. (1,620 yd.) white, CC
Size J crochet hook or size to
 obtain gauge

Finished Size

Approximately 42" x 65"

Gauge

In pat, 20 sc and 12 rows = 5"

Pattern Stitch

Puff: (Yo, insert hook in st indicated, yo and pull up lp) 4 times, yo and pull through all 9 lps on hook, ch 1.

Note: To change colors, work last yo of prev st with new color, dropping prev color to ws of work.

With MC, ch 171.
Row 1 (rs): Sc in 2nd ch from hook, sk 1 ch, * sc in next 9 chs, 5 sc in next ch, sc in next 9 chs, sk 1 ch; rep from * across to last ch, sc in last ch.
Row 2: Ch 1, turn; sc in first sc, sk 1 sc, * sc in next 10 sc, 3 sc in next sc, sc in next 10 sc **, sk next 2 sc; rep from * across, ending last rep at **, sc in last sc, change to CC.
Row 3: With CC, ch 3, turn; sk first 2 sc, * puff in next sc, (sk 1 sc, puff in next sc) 10 times **, sk 2 sc; rep from * across, ending last

rep at **, dc in last sc.
Row 4: Ch 1, turn; sc in top of first puff, sc in sp before next puff, * (sc in top of next puff, sc in sp before next puff) 4 times, 5 sc in top of next puff, sc in sp before next puff, (sc in top of next puff, sc in sp before next puff) 4 times **, sk 2 puffs, sc in sp before next puff; rep from * across, ending last rep at **, sc in top of tch, change to MC.
Row 5: Ch 1, turn; sc in first sc, sk 1 sc, * sc in next 10 sc, 3 sc in next sc, sc in next 10 sc **, sk next 2 sc; rep from * across, ending last rep at **, sc in top of tch.
Rows 6–13: Rep rows 2–5 twice.
Rows 14–20: With MC, rep row 5, 7 times, changing to CC in last st of last row.
Rows 21–28: With CC, rep row 5, 8 times, changing to MC in last st of last row.

Row 29: With MC, rep row 5.
Rows 30–42: Rep rows 2–14 once, changing to CC in last st of last row.
Rows 43–62: With CC, rep row 5, 20 times, changing to MC in last st of last row.
Rows 63–94: Rep rows 2–20 once, then rep rows 2–14 once, changing to CC in last st of last row.
Rows 95–114: With CC, rep row 5, 20 times, changing to MC in last st of last row.
Rows 115–155: Rep rows 2–42 once; do not change colors or fasten off after last row.

Border

Row 1 (rs): With rs facing and MC and working along left edge of afghan, * sc evenly across to next CC section, change to CC, sc evenly across to next MC section, change to MC; rep from * across to next corner; fasten off.
Row 2: With rs facing, join MC to bottom right corner of afghan with sl st, ch 1, sc in same st; working along right edge of afghan, * sc evenly across to next CC section, change to CC, sc evenly across to next MC section, change to MC; rep from * across to next corner; fasten off.

Project was stitched with Wool-Ease: Black Frost #502 and White Frost #501.

Cables and Lace

The double crochet lace panels are manly enough for my husband's study when stitched in an earthy brown. And they set off the cream cables beautifully.

Materials
Worsted-weight alpaca-wool-acrylic blend yarn, approximately:
17½ oz. (1,070 yd.) ecru, MC
22¾ oz. (1,395 yd.) brown, CC
Size J crochet hook or size to obtain gauge

Finished Size
Approximately 46" x 63"
(37" x 54" without border)

Gauge
Cable Strip = 5½" x 54"
Lace Strip = 2¼" x 54"

Pattern Stitches
Front Post dc (FPdc): Yo, insert hook from front to back around post of st indicated, yo and pull up lp, (yo and pull through 2 lps) twice; sk st behind FPdc.

Back Post dc (BPdc): Yo, insert hook from back to front around post of st indicated, yo and pull up lp, (yo and pull through 2 lps) twice; sk st behind BPdc.

Front Post tr (FPtr): Yo twice, insert hook from front to back around post of next st, yo and pull up lp, (yo and pull through 2 lps) 3 times.

Cable Strip (Make 4.)
With MC, ch 22.
Row 1 (rs): Dc in 4th ch from hook and in next 2 chs, * sk next 2 chs, tr in next 2 chs, working in front of last 2 sts, tr in 2 sk chs, dc in next 4 dc; rep from * once: 20 sts. *Note:* Mark last row as rs.

Row 2: Ch 3 [counts as first dc throughout], turn; sk first st, dc in next 3 sts, BPdc around next 4 sts, dc in next 4 sts, BPdc around next 4 sts, dc in last 3 sts, dc in top of tch.

Row 3: Ch 3, turn; sk first st, dc in next st, * sk next 2 sts, FPtr around next 2 sts, working behind last 2 sts, dc in 2 sk sts [back twist made]; sk next 2 sts, dc in next 2 sts, working in front of last 2 sts, FPtr around 2 sk sts [front twist made]; rep from * once, dc in last 2 sts.

Row 4: Ch 3, turn; sk first st, dc in next st, BPdc around next 2 sts, dc in next 4 sts, BPdc around next 4 sts, dc in next 4 sts, BPdc around next 2 sts, dc in last 2 sts.

(continued)

Project was stitched with Al•Pa•Ka: Natural #98 and Mink Brown #127.

Row 5: Ch 3, turn; sk first st, dc in next st, FPdc around next 2 sts, dc in next 4 sts, sk next 2 sts, FPtr around next 2 sts, working in front of last 2 sts, FPtr around 2 sk sts [front cable made]; dc in next 4 sts, FPdc around next 2 sts, dc in last 2 sts.
Row 6: Rep row 4.

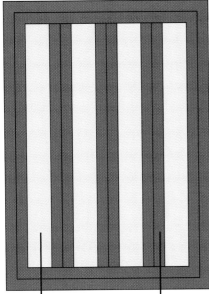

Cable Strip   *Lace Strip*
Assembly Diagram

Row 7: Ch 3, turn; sk first st, dc in next st, (front twist over next 4 sts, back twist over next 4 sts) twice, dc in last 2 sts.
Row 8: Rep row 2.
Row 9: Ch 3, turn; sk first st, dc in next 3 sts, (front cable over next 4 sts, dc in next 4 sts) twice.
Rows 10–106: Rep rows 2–9, 12 times, then rep row 2 once. Fasten off after last row.

Lace Strip (Make 6.)

With CC, ch 4, join with sl st to form ring.
Row 1 (rs): Ch 3 [counts as first dc throughout], 3 dc in ring, ch 2, 4 dc in ring.
Note: Mark last row as rs.
Row 2: Ch 3, turn; (3 dc, ch 2, 3 dc) in ch-2 sp, dc in last dc.
   Rep row 2 until piece measures approximately 54"; fasten off.

Assembly

Referring to ***Assembly Diagram,*** join 1 Lace Strip to 1 Cable Strip

as folls: With rs facing, join CC to bottom right corner of Cable Strip with sl st, * ch 1, sc in corresponding row of Lace Strip, ch 1, sc in end of next row of Cable Strip; rep from * across to next corner; fasten off.
   Rep to join rem strips.

Border

Rnd 1: With CC, work as for Lace Strip until piece measures approximately 202". With rs facing, join CC in corner of afghan with sl st, * ch 1, sc in corresponding row of Border Strip, ch 1, sc in next row of afghan; rep from * around; fasten off. Whipstitch border seam tog.
Rnd 2: With CC, work as for Lace Strip until piece measures approximately 234". With rs facing, join CC in corner of afghan with sl st, * ch 1, sc in corresponding row of Border Strip, ch 1, sc in next row of afghan; rep from * around; fasten off. Whipstitch border seam tog.

Tree of Life

Vertical and diagonal post stitches branch out to form a dynamic pattern. Be sure to work the post stitches loosely so that they lie flat.

Materials

Worsted-weight wool-blend yarn, approximately:
54 oz. (3,550 yd.) blue
Sizes H and J crochet hooks or sizes to obtain gauge

Finished Size

Approximately 50" x 58"

Gauge

In pat with larger hook, 14 sts and 18 rows = 4"

Pattern Stitches

Front Post dc (FPdc): Yo, insert hook from front to back around post of st indicated, yo and pull up lp, (yo and pull through 2 lps) twice; sk st behind FPdc.

Three Front Post cluster (3FPcl): Yo, insert hook from front to back around st indicated, yo and pull up lp, (yo insert hook from front to back around next st, yo and pull up lp) twice, yo and pull through all 4 lps on hook; sk st behind 3FPcl.

Two Front Post cluster (2FPcl): Yo, insert hook from front to back around st indicated, yo and pull up lp, yo insert hook from front to back around next st, yo and pull up lp, yo and pull through all 3 lps on hook; sk st behind 2FPcl.

With larger hook, ch 175.

Row 1 (rs): Sc in 2nd ch from hook and in ea ch across: 174 sc.

Row 2 and all Even Rows: Ch 1, turn; sc in first st and in ea st across: 174 sc.

Row 3: Ch 1, turn; sc in first sc, FPdc around next 2 sts 2 rows below, * sc in next sc, FPdc around st 2 rows below last sc, sc in next 5 sc, FPdc around next

st 2 rows below, sc in next 5 sc, sk next st, FPdc around next st 2 rows below, sc in st above last FPdc, FPdc around next 2 sts 2 rows below, sc in next 6 sc, sk next st, FPdc around next st 2 rows below, dc in sp before next st 2 rows below, FPdc around next st 2 rows below, sc in next 6 sc, FPdc around next 2 sts 2 rows below; rep from * across to last sc, sc in last sc.

Row 5: Ch 1, turn; sc in first sc, FPdc around next 2 FPdc, * sc in next 2 sc, FPdc around next FPdc, (sc in next 4 sc, FPdc around next FPdc) twice, sc in next 2 sc, FPdc around next 2 FPdc, sc in next 5 sts, FPdc around next FPdc, sc in next st, FPdc around next dc, sc in next sc, FPdc around next FPdc, sc in next 5 sts, FPdc around next 2 FPdc; rep from * across to last sc, sc in last sc.

Row 7: Ch 1, turn; sc in first sc,

FPdc around next 2 FPdc, * (sc in next 3 sc, FPdc around next FPdc) 4 times, FPdc around next FPdc, sc in next 4 sc, FPdc around next FPdc, (sc in next 2 sc, FPdc around next FPdc) twice, sc in next 4 sc, FPdc around next 2 FPdc; rep from * across to last sc, sc in last sc.

Row 9: Ch 1, turn; sc in first sc, FPdc around next 2 FPdc, * sc in next 4 sc, (FPdc around next FPdc, sc in next 2 sc) twice, FPdc around next FPdc, sc in next 4 sc, FPdc around next 2 FPdc, (sc in next 3 sc, FPdc around next FPdc) 4 times, FPdc around next FPdc; rep from * across to last sc, sc in last sc.

Row 11: Ch 1, turn; sc in first sc, FPdc around next 2 FPdc, * sc in next 5 sc, (FPdc around next FPdc, sc in next sc) twice, FPdc around next FPdc, sc in next 5 sc, FPdc around next 2 FPdc, sc in

Project was stitched with Wool-Ease: Blue Mist #115.

next 2 sc, FPdc around next FPdc, (sc in next 4 sc, FPdc around next FPdc) twice, sc in next 2 sc, FPdc around next 2 FPdc; rep from * across to last sc, sc in last sc.

Row 13: Ch 1, turn; sc in first sc, FPdc around next 2 FPdc, * sc in next 6 sc, FPdc around next 3 FPdc, sc in next 6 sc, FPdc around next 2 FPdc, sc in next sc, (FPdc around next FPdc, sc in next 5 sc) twice, FPdc around next FPdc, sc in next sc, FPdc around next 2 FPdc; rep from * across to last sc, sc in last sc.

Row 15: Ch 1, turn; sc in first sc, FPdc around next 2 FPdc, * sc in next 7 sc, beg 3FPcl around next FPdc, sc in next 7 sc, FPdc around next 3 FPdc, (sc in next 6 sc, FPdc around next FPdc) twice, FPdc around next 2 FPdc; rep from * across to last sc, sc in last sc.

Row 17: Ch 1, turn; sc in first sc, FPdc around next 2 FPdc, * sc in next 7 sc, FPdc around 3FPcl, sc in next 7 sc, FPdc around next FPdc, beg 2FPcl around next FPdc, sc in next 7 sc, FPdc around next FPdc, sc in next 7 sc, beg 2FPcl around next FPdc, FPdc around next FPdc; rep from * across to last sc, sc in last sc.

Row 19: Ch 1, turn; sc in first sc, FPdc around next 2 FPdc, * sc in next sc, FPdc around st 2 rows below last sc, sc in next 5 sc, FPdc around next FPdc, sc in next 5 sc, sk next st, FPdc around next st 2 rows below, sc in st above last FPdc, FPdc around next 2 FPdc, sc in next 6 sc, sk next st, 3 FPdc around next FPdc, sc in next 6 sc, FPdc around next 2 FPdc; rep from * across to last sc, sc in last sc.

Rows 20–257: Rep rows 4–19, 14 times, then rep rows 4–17 once; do not fasten off after last row.

Border

With smaller hook and rs facing, 3 sc in same st, sc evenly across to next corner, * 3 sc in corner, sc evenly across to next corner; rep from * around; join with sl st to beg sc; fasten off.

*When checking your gauge on heavily textured afghans, such as the **Tree of Life,** measure your stitches on the wrong side of the piece. This way post stitches or puffs won't distort your measurements.*

Shadow Box

Use several shades of a color to create the appearance of depth in each block. For added interest, join the blocks on point so that they form a zigzag edge.

Materials
Worsted-weight acrylic yarn, approximately:
18 oz. (940 yd.) burgundy, MC
18 oz. (940 yd.) dark rose, A
12 oz. (625 yd.) rose, B
12 oz. (625 yd.) cream, C
Size K crochet hook or size to obtain gauge
Yarn needle

Finished Size
Approximately 56" x 70"

Gauge
12 sc and 14 rows = 4"

Note: To change colors, work last yo of prev st with new color, dropping prev color to ws of work. Do not carry yarn across row.

Block (Make 32.)
With MC, ch 31.
Row 1 (rs): Sc in 2nd ch from hook and in ea ch across: 30 sc.
Note: Mark last row as rs.
Rows 2 and 3: Ch 1, turn; sc in ea ch across.
Rows 4–11: Ch 1, turn; sc in first 3 sc, change to A, sc in next 24 sc, change to MC, sc in last 3 sc.
Row 12: Ch 1, turn; sc in first 3 sc, change to B, sc in next 17 sc, change to A, sc in next 7 sc, change to MC, sc in last 3 sc.
Row 13: Ch 1, turn; sc in first 3 sc, change to A, sc in next 7 sc,

change to B, sc in next 17 sc, change to MC, sc in last 3 sc.
Rows 14–18: Rep rows 12 and 13 alternately, ending with row 12.
Row 19: Ch 1, turn; sc in first 3 sc, change to A, sc in next 7 sc, change to B, sc in next 6 sc, change to C, sc in next 11 sc, change to MC, sc in last 3 sc.
Row 20: Ch 1, turn; sc in first 3 sc, change to C, sc in next 11 sc, change to B, sc in next 6 sc, change to A, sc in next 7 sc, change to MC, sc in last 3 sc.
Rows 21–31: Rep rows 19 and 20 alternately, ending with row 19.
Rows 32–34: Ch 1, turn; sc in ea sc across; fasten off after last row.

Assembly
Referring to *Assembly Diagram,* whipstitch blocks tog.

Border
With rs facing and referring to *Assembly Diagram,* join MC in corner with sl st, ch 1, sc in same st, * (sc evenly across to next

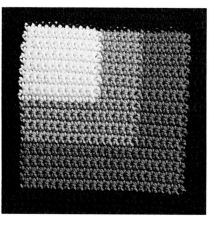

inner corner, sk 2 sts, sc evenly across to next outer corner, 3 sc in outer corner) 4 times, sc evenly across to next outer corner, 3 sc in outer corner, (sc evenly across to next inner corner, sk 2 sts, sc evenly across to next outer corner, 3 sc in outer corner) 3 times, sc evenly across to next outer corner, 3 sc in outer corner; rep from * around; join with sl st to beg sc; fasten off.

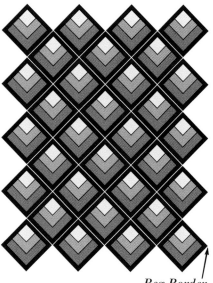

Assembly Diagram

Beg Border

Project was stitched with Keepsake Sayelle: Burgundy #142, Dark Mauve #141, Light Mauve #140, and Cream #98.

Checks and Stripes

Chunky yarn and double crochet stitches make quick work of this sweet baby afghan. Keep it simple with three colors or add a new color with each strip.

Materials

Chunky-weight brushed acrylic yarn, approximately:
6 oz. (270 yd.) white, MC
9 oz. (405 yd.) aqua, A
9 oz. (405 yd.) lavender, B
Sizes H and J crochet hooks or sizes to obtain gauge

Finished Size

Approximately 36" x 36"

Gauge

13 dc and 7 rows = 4"

Note: To change colors, work last yo of prev st with new color, dropping prev color to ws of work. Carry yarn not in use loosely across row.

With larger hook and B, ch 112.
Row 1 (rs): Dc in 4th ch from hook and in next 3 chs, * change to A, dc in next 3 chs, change to B, dc in next 3 chs; rep from * across, to last 4 dc, change to A, dc in last 4 chs, change to B: 110 dc.
Rows 2 and 3: With B, ch 3 [counts as first dc throughout], turn; dc in next 3 dc, * change to A, dc in next 3 dc, change to B, dc in next 3 dc; rep from * across to last 4 dc, change to A, dc in last 4 dc, change to B: 110 dc.
Row 4 (ws): With B, ch 3, turn; dc in next 3 dc, * change to A, dc in next 3 dc, change to B, dc in next 3 dc; rep from * across to last 4 dc, change to A, dc in last 4 dc, change to MC.
Row 5: With MC, ch 1, turn; sc in ea dc across: 110 sc.
Row 6: Ch 1, turn; sc in ea sc across, change to B in last st; fasten off MC.
Row 7: With B, ch 3, turn; working in both lps, dc in next 3 sts, * change to A, dc in next 3 sts, change to B, dc in next 3 sts; rep from * across to last 4 sts, change to A, dc in last 4 sts.
Row 8: With A, ch 3, turn; dc in next 3 dc, * change to B, dc in next 3 dc, change to A, dc in next 3 dc; rep from * across to last 4 dc, change to B, dc in last 4 sc.
Rows 9 and 10: Rep rows 7 and 8 once, changing to MC in last st of last row.
Row 11: Rep rows 5.
Row 12: Ch 1, turn; sc in ea sc across, change to A in last st; fasten off MC.
Row 13: With A, ch 3, turn; dc in ea dc across, change to B in last st.

Row 14: With B, ch 3 turn; dc in ea dc across, change to A in last st.
Row 15: Rep row 13.
Row 16: With B, ch 3 turn; dc in ea dc across, change to MC in last st.
Rows 17 and 18: Rep rows 5 and 6.
Row 19: With B, ch 3, turn; dc in next 3 dc, * change to A, dc in next 3 dc, change to B, dc in next 3 dc; rep from * across to last 4 dc, change to A, dc in last 4 dc.
Rows 20–70: Rep rows 2–19 twice, then rep rows 2–16 once; fasten off after last row.

Border

Rnd 1 (rs): With rs facing and smaller hook, join MC in top right corner with sl st, ch 1, sc in same st and in ea st across to corner, * 3 sc in corner; sc evenly across to next corner, rep from * around; join with sl st to beg sc.
Rnd 2: Ch 1, working in bk lps only, sc in ea sc across to corner, * 3 sc in corner, sc in ea sc across to next corner; rep from * around; join with sl st to beg sc; fasten off.

Project was stitched with Jiffy: White #100, Aqua #102, and Lilac #144.

Yellow Bows

Bring a ray of sunshine into any room with a bunch of bright bow-shaped clusters.

Materials

Worsted-weight acrylic yarn, approximately:
54 oz. (2,810 yd.) yellow
Size H crochet hook or size to obtain gauge

Finished Size

Approximately 53" x 70"

Gauge

13 hdc and 9 rows = 4"

Pattern Stitch

Cl: Ch 4, (yo, insert hook in 4th ch from hook, yo and pull up lp) twice, yo and pull through all 5 lps on hook.

Ch 167.

Row 1 (ws): Hdc in 2nd ch from hook and in ea ch across: 166 hdc.

Rows 2 and 3: Ch 2, turn; hdc in first hdc and in ea hdc across.

Row 4 (rs): Ch 2, turn; hdc in first 8 hdc, * cl, ch 1, cl, sk next 6 hdc, hdc in next 6 hdc; rep from * across to last 2 hdc, hdc in last 2 hdc.

Row 5: Ch 2, turn; hdc in first 8 hdc, * cl, sc in next ch-1, cl, sk next cl, hdc in next 6 hdc; rep from * across to last 2 hdc, hdc in last 2 hdc.

Row 6: Ch 2, turn; hdc in first 8 hdc, * ch 6, sk 2 cls, hdc in next 6 hdc; rep from * across to last 2 hdc, hdc in last 2 hdc.

Row 7: Ch 2, turn; hdc in ea hdc and ea ch across: 166 hdc.

Rows 8-11: Rep row 2, 4 times.

Row 12: Ch 2, turn; hdc in first 2 hdc, * cl, ch 1, cl, sk next 6 hdc **, hdc in next 6 hdc; rep from * across, ending last rep at **, hdc in last 2 hdc.

Row 13: Ch 2, turn; hdc in first 2 hdc, * cl, sc in next ch-1, cl, sk next cl **, hdc in next 6 hdc; rep from * across, ending last rep at **, hdc in last 2 hdc.

Row 14: Ch 2, turn; hdc in first 2 hdc, * ch 6, sk 2 cls **, hdc in next 6 hdc; rep from * across, ending last rep at **, hdc in last 2 hdc.

Rows 15-17: Rep rows 7-9.

Rows 18-153: Rep rows 2-17, 8 times, then rep rows 2-9 once; do not fasten off.

Border

Ch 1, turn; hdc in first hdc and in ea hdc across to corner, * 3 hdc in corner, hdc evenly across to next corner; rep from * around; join with sl st to beg hdc; fasten off.

Project was stitched with Keepsake Sayelle: Goldenrod #187.

Victorian Fringe

On chilly mornings wrap up in elegance with this soft, feminine throw. Extralong fringe and lace drape gently from each edge.

Materials
Worsted-weight mohair-blend yarn, approximately:
37½ oz. (3,330 yd.) ecru
Size J crochet hook or size to obtain gauge
6½ yd. 5"-wide ecru lace
Sewing needle and thread
Pins
4 yd. 1⅜"-wide ecru satin ribbon
4 safety pins

Finished Size
Approximately 44" x 62", without fringe

Gauge
In pat, 17 sts and 18 rows = 4"

Ch 188.
Row 1 (rs): Sc in 2nd ch from hook, (ch 1, sk 1 ch, sc in next ch) across: 94 sc.
Row 2: Ch 1, turn; sc in first sc and first ch-1 sp, (ch 1, sk next sc, sc in next ch-1 sp) across to last sc, sc in last sc: 95 sc.
Row 3: Ch 1, turn; sc in first sc, (ch 1, sk next sc, sc in next ch-1 sp) across.

Rep rows 2 and 3 alternately until piece measures approximately 62"; fasten off after last row.

Fringe
For ea tassel, referring to page 143 of General Directions, cut 2 (16") lengths of yarn. Working across short ends, knot 1 tassel in every other st. Working across long edges, knot 1 tassel in every other row.

With rs facing, pin lace along afghan edges, mitering corners. Sew lace to afghan; sew short seam to join lace.

Cut 4 (34") lengths of ribbon. Tie ea length in bow and pin 1 bow to ea corner of afghan with safety pin.

Attach the ribbons with safety pins so that you can remove them before washing the afghan.

Project was stitched with Imagine: Fisherman #99.

Rosebud Clusters

Choose a cheery color and crochet an afghan full of flowers.
Finish it with cluster and picot edging.

Materials

Worsted-weight wool-blend yarn, approximately:
51 oz. (3,350 yd.) dark rose
Sizes H and J crochet hooks or sizes to obtain gauge

Finished Size

Approximately 50" x 58"

Gauge

In pat with larger hook, 14 sts and 16 rows = 4"

Pattern Stitches

Puff: (Yo, insert hook in st indicated and pull up lp) 3 times, yo and pull through all 7 lps on hook.

Long dc (Ldc): Yo, insert hook in st indicated, pull up ¾" lp, (yo and draw through 2 lps) twice; sk st behind Ldc.

Front Post dc (FPdc): Yo, insert hook from front to back around post of st indicated, yo and pull up lp, (yo and pull through 2 lps) twice; sk st behind FPdc.

Back Post dc (BPdc): Yo, insert hook from back to front around post of st indicated, yo and pull up lp, (yo and pull through 2 lps) twice; sk st behind BPdc.

Picot: Ch 2, sl st in 2nd ch from hook.

With larger hook, ch 164.
Row 1 (rs): Sc in 2nd ch from hook and in ea ch across: 163 sc.
Rows 2-4: Ch 1, turn; sc in first sc and in ea st across: 163 sc.

Row 5: Ch 1, turn; sc in first 5 sc, * sk next sc, 3 Ldc in next sc 2 rows below **, sc in next 7 sc; rep from * across, ending last rep at **, sc in last 5 sc.
Row 6: Rep row 2.
Row 7: Ch 1, turn; sc in first 4 sc, * (FPdc around next Ldc, sc in next st) 3 times, sc in next 4 sc; rep from * across.
Row 8: Ch 1, turn; sc in first 3 sc, (puff in next st, sc in next 4 sts) across.
Row 9: Ch 1, turn; sc in first 6 sts, (FPdc around next FPdc, sc in next 9 sts) across to last 7 sts, FPdc around next FPdc, sc in last 6 sts.
Row 10: Ch 1, turn; sc in first 5 sc, (puff in next st, sc in next 9 sts) across to last 8 sts, puff in next st, sc in last 7 sts.
Rows 11 and 12: Rep row 2 twice.
Row 13: Ch 1, turn; sc in first 10 sc, * sk next sc, 3 Ldc in next st 2 rows below **, sc in next 7 sc; rep from * across, ending last rep at **, sc in last 10 sc.
Row 14: Rep row 2.
Row 15: Ch 1, turn; sc in first 9 sc, * (FPdc around next Ldc, sc in next st) 3 times **, sc in next 4 sc; rep from * across, ending last rep at **, sc in last 8 sc.
Row 16: Ch 1, turn; sc in first 8 sc, (puff in next st, sc in next 4 sts) across to last 10 sts, puff in next st, sc in last 9 sc.
Row 17: Ch 1, turn; sc in first 11 sts, (FPdc around next FPdc, sc in next 9 sts) across to last 12 sts, FPdc around next FPdc, sc in last 11 sts.

Row 18: Ch 1, turn; sc in first 10 sc, (puff in next st, sc in next 9 sts) across to last 13 sts, puff in next st, sc in last 12 sts.
Rows 19 and 20: Rep row 2 twice.
Rows 21-220: Rep rows 5-20, 12 times, then rep rows 5-12 once; do not fasten off.

Border

Rnd 1 (rs): With smaller hook, ch 1, turn; 3 sc in first sc, sc in ea sc across to corner, * 3 sc in corner, sc evenly across to next corner; rep from * around; join with sl st to beg sc.
Rnd 2: Ch 1, turn; sc in first sc, * (puff in next sc, sc in next sc) across to next corner, (sc, puff, sc) in corner; rep from * around; join with sl st to beg sc.
Rnd 3: Ch 1, turn; sc in first sc, * 3 sc in corner, sc in ea st across to next corner; rep from * around; join with sl st to beg sc.
Rnd 4: Ch 1, do not turn; sc in first sc, (ch 5, sk next 3 sc, sc in next sc) around; join with ch 5, sl st to beg sc.
Rnd 5: Ch 1, do not turn; sc in first sc, * (2 sc, picot, 2 sc) in next ch-5 sp, sc in next sc; rep from * around; join with sl st to beg sc; fasten off.

Project was stitched with Wool-Ease: Strawberry Heather #103.

Tyrolean Christmas

Bring some old-world style to your holidays with this handsome afghan. The designs are crocheted separately and then appliquéd. Fill a matching stocking with surprises from Santa Claus.

Afghan

Materials
Worsted-weight wool-blend
  yarn, approximately:
33 oz. (2,170 yd.) cream, MC
18 oz. (1,185 yd.) red, A
18 oz. (1,185 yd.) green, B
Sizes H and I crochet hooks or
  sizes to obtain gauge
Yarn needle

Finished Size
Approximately 52" x 63"

Gauge
With larger hook, 14 sc and 18
rows = 4"

Pattern Stitches
Bobble: (Yo, insert hook in st indicated, yo and pull up lp) 5 times, yo and pull through all 11 lps on hook.

Puff: (Yo, insert hook in st indicated, yo and pull up lp) 3 times, yo and pull through all 7 lps on hook.

Note: To change colors, work last yo of prev st with new color, dropping prev color to ws of work. Carry yarn loosely across row.

With larger hook and B, ch 176.
Row 1 (rs): Sc in 2nd ch from hook and in ea ch across: 175 sc.

Rows 2 and 3: Ch 1, turn; sc in first st and in ea st across: 175 sc.
Row 4: Ch 1, turn; sc in first 7 sc, * change to MC, bobble in next sc, change to B **, sc in next 9 sc; rep from * across, ending last rep at **, sc in last 7 sc.
Row 5: Rep row 2.
Row 6: Ch 1, turn; sc in first 6 sc, * (change to MC, bobble in next sc, change to B, sc in next sc) twice **, sc in next 6 sc; rep from * across, ending last rep at **, sc in last 5 sc.
Row 7: Rep row 2.
Row 8: Rep row 4.
Rows 9–11: Rep row 2, 3 times; fasten off after last row.
Row 12 (rs): With rs facing, join A in top right corner with sl st, ch 1, sc in same st and in ea st across: 175 sc.
Row 13: Ch 1, turn; sc in first sc, (puff in next sc, sc in next sc) across to last sc, sc in last sc.
Row 14: With A, rep row 2; fasten off.
Row 15 (rs): With rs facing, join MC in top right corner with sl st, ch 1, sc in same st and in ea st across: 175 sc.
Rows 16–48: With MC, rep row 2, 33 times, changing to A in last st of last row.
Row 49: With A, rep row 2.
Rows 50 and 51: Rep rows 13 and 14.
Row 52 (rs): With rs facing, join B in top right corner with sl st, ch 1, sc in same st and in ea st across: 175 sc.

Rows 53–266: Rep rows 2–52, 4 times, then rep rows 2–11 once; fasten off after last row.

Border
Rnd 1 (rs): With rs facing and smaller hook, join A to top right corner with sl st, ch 1, sc in same st and in ea st across to corner, * 3 sc in corner, sc evenly across to next corner; rep from * around; join with sl st to beg sc.
Rnd 2 (ws): Ch 1, turn; sc in first sc, * (puff in next sc, sc in next sc) across to corner, (puff, sc, puff) in corner; rep from * around; join with sl st to beg sc.
Rnd 3: Ch 1, turn; sc in first sc and in ea st across to corner, * 3 sc in corner, sc in ea st across to next corner; rep from * around; join with sl st to beg sc; fasten off.
Rnd 4: With rs facing and smaller hook, join B to top right corner with sl st, ch 1, sc in same st, * ch 2, sl st in 2nd ch from hook, sk next sc, sl st in next sc; rep from * around; join with sl st to beg sc; fasten off.

Embroidery
Using photo as placement guide and referring to stitch diagrams on page 142, work 3 French knots and 4 lazy daisy stitches in ea bobble grp with A.

(continued)

Project was stitched with Wool-Ease: Ivory Sprinkles #97, Red Sprinkles #112, and Hunter Green Sprinkles #131.

Heart (Make 20.)

With smaller hook and A, ch 3.

Row 1 (rs): 2 dc in 3rd ch from hook.

Note: Mark last row as rs.

Row 2: Ch 3 [counts as first dc throughout], turn; 2 dc in first dc, ch 1, sk next dc, 3 dc in top of beg ch.

Row 3: Ch 3, turn; 2 dc in first dc, ch 1, sk next dc, dc in next dc, dc in next ch-1 sp, dc in next dc, ch 1, sk next dc, 3 dc in last dc.

Rows 4–7: Ch 3, turn; 2 dc in first dc, * ch 1, sk next dc **, dc in next dc, dc in next ch-1 sp, dc in next dc; rep from * across, ending last rep at **, 3 dc in last dc.

Row 8: Ch 3, turn; sk first 2 dc, (dc in next dc, dc in next ch-1 sp, dc in next dc, ch 1, sk next dc) twice, dc in next dc, dc in next ch-1 sp, dc in next dc, leave rem 11 dc unworked.

Row 9: Ch 3, turn; sk first 2 dc, * dc in next dc, dc in next ch-1 sp, dc in next dc, sk next dc **, ch 1; rep from * to ** once, dc in last dc; fasten off.

Row 10 (ws): With ws facing, join A in 2nd unworked dc on row 8 with sl st, ch 3, (dc in next ch-1 sp, dc in next dc, ch 1, sk next dc, dc in next dc) twice, dc in next ch-1 sp, dc in next dc, sk next dc, dc in last dc.

Row 11: Rep row 9.

Edging

With rs facing and smaller hook, join A in beg ch with sl st, ch 3, sl st in end of next row, (ch 3, sl st) evenly around; join with sl st to beg sl st; fasten off.

Vine (Make 40.)

With smaller hook and B, ch 64; sl st in 2nd ch from hook, * ch 2, sl st in 2nd ch from hook, sk next ch, sl st in next ch; rep from * across; fasten off.

Assembly

Referring to photo for placement, sew 4 Hearts evenly sp in ea MC panel. Sew 2 Vines around ea Heart.

Stocking

Materials

Worsted-weight wool-blend yarn, approximately:
3 oz. (200 yd.) cream, MC
3 oz. (200 yd.) red, A
3 oz. (200 yd.) green, B
Sizes H and I crochet hooks or sizes to obtain gauge
Yarn needle

Finished Size

Approximately 16½"

Gauge

With larger hook, 14 sc and 18 rows = 4"

Leg

With larger hook and MC, ch 46.

Row 1: Sc in 2nd ch from hook and in ea ch across: 45 sc.

Row 2: Ch 1, turn; sc in first sc and in ea sc across: 45 sc.

Rep row 2 until piece measures approximately 7"; fasten off.

Heel

Row 1 (rs): Sk 34 sc, with larger hook, join B in next sc with sl st, ch 1, sc in same sc and in last 10 sc; fold piece in half so ends meet, sc in first 10 sc [joining made]: 21 sc.

Row 2: Ch 1, turn; sc in first 14 sc, leave rem 7 sc unworked.

Row 3: Ch 1, turn; sc in first 7 sc, leave rem 7 sc unworked.

Row 4: Ch 1, turn; sc in first sc and in ea sc across, sc in next sc on row 3: 8 sc.

Row 5: Ch 1, turn; sc in first sc and in ea sc across, sc in next sc on row 2: 9 sc.

Rows 6–17: Rep rows 4 and 5, times; fasten off after last row.

Foot

Row 1: With rs facing and larger hook, sk first 11 sc on row 17 of heel, join MC to next sc with sl st, ch 1, sc in same st and in next 9 sc, sk first 2 sc on last row of Leg, sc in next 20 sc, sk last 2 sc on last row of Leg, sc in next 11 sc on row 17 of heel: 41 sc.

Row 2: Ch 1, turn; sc in first 10 sc; (insert hook in next sc, yo and pull up lp) twice, yo and pull through all 3 lps on hook [dec made]; sc in next 18 sc, dec, sc in last 9 sc: 39 sc.

Row 3: Ch 1, turn; sc in first sc and in ea sc across: 39 sc.

Rep row 3 until Foot measures approximately 3¾" from Heel, changing to B in last st of last row.

Toe

Row 1: With B, ch 1, turn; sc in first 18 sc, dec, sc last 19 sc: 38 sc.

Row 2: Ch 1, turn; dec in first 2 sc, sc in next 15 sc, dec in next 2 sc, leave rem sc unworked: 17 sc.

Rows 3–8: Ch 1, turn; dec in first 2 sc, sc in ea sc across to last 2 sc, dec in last 2 sc; fasten off.

Row 9: With larger hook, join B in last sc on row 1 with sl st, ch 1, dec in first 2 sc, sc in next 15 sc, dec in last 2 sc: 17 sc.

Rows 10–15: Rep rows 3–8 once.

Rows 12–14: Rep row 5, 3 times; fasten off after last row.

Row 15: With rs facing and larger hook, join A in first sc with sl st, ch 1, sc in first sc and in ea sc across.

Rows 16 and 17: Work as for rows 13 and 14 of Afghan.

Row 18: With rs facing and larger hook, join B in first sc with sl st, ch 1, sc in same st, * ch 2, sl st in 2nd ch from hook, sk next sc, sl st in next sc; rep from * across to last sc, ch 10; join with sl st to beg sc [hanger made]; fasten off.

Heart

With smaller hook and A, ch 3.

Rows 1–5: Work as for rows 1–5 of Afghan Heart.

Row 6: Ch 3, turn; sk first 2 dc, * dc in next dc, dc in next ch-1 sp, dc in next dc **, ch 1; rep from * to ** once, leave rem 8 dc unworked.

Row 7: Ch 3, turn; sk first 2 dc, dc in next dc, dc in next ch-1 sp, dc in next dc, sk next dc, dc in last dc; fasten off.

Row 8 (ws): With ws facing, join A in 2nd unworked dc on row 5 with sl st, ch 3, * dc in next ch-1 sp, dc in next dc **, ch 1, sk next dc, dc in next dc; rep from * to ** once, sk next dc, dc in last dc.

Row 9: Rep row 7.

Edging
Work as for Afghan Heart Edging.

Vine (Make 2.)

With smaller hook and B, ch 40.
Work as for Afghan Vine.

Embroidery

Work as for Afghan Embroidery.

Assembly

Sew Heart on front of Leg. Sew 2 Vines around Heart. With rs facing, whipstitch seams tog along Leg, Foot, and sides of Heel.

Cuff

Row 1: With rs facing and larger hook, join A in beg ch of Leg with sl st, ch 1, sc in same st and in ea st across: 45 sc.

Rows 2 and 3: Work as for rows 13 and 14 of Afghan.

Row 4: With rs facing and larger hook, join B in first sc with sl st, ch 1, sc in first sc and in ea sc across.

Rows 5 and 6: Ch 1, turn; sc in first st and in ea st across: 175 sc.

Row 7: Ch 1, turn; sc in first 7 sc, * change to MC, bobble in next sc, change to B, sc in next 7 sc **, change to MC, bobble in next sc, change to B, sc in next 13 sc; rep from * to ** twice.

Row 8: Rep row 5.

Row 9: Ch 1, turn; sc in first 6 sc, * (change to MC, bobble in next sc, change to B, sc in next sc) twice, sc in next 4 sc **; rep from * to ** once, sc in next 7 sc; rep from * to ** twice more, sc in last sc.

Rows 10 and 11: Rep rows 6 and 7.

Project was stitched with Wool-Ease: Ivory Sprinkles #97, Red Sprinkles #112, and Hunter Green Sprinkles #131.

Santa Fe Fringe

Tie silver conchos and turquoise beads to this Southwestern favorite.

Materials
Worsted-weight alpaca-wool-acrylic blend yarn, approximately:

45½ oz. (2,785 yd.) brown

Size H crochet hook or size to obtain gauge

20 (1½"-diameter) silver conchos

Approximately 1,250 (6-mm) turquoise pony beads

Finished Size
Approximately 49" x 52", without fringe

Gauge
In pat, 20 dc and 8 rows = 5"

Pattern Stitches
Dec: Yo, insert hook in st indicated, yo and pull up lp, yo and pull through 2 lps, sk 1 st, yo, insert hook in next st, yo and pull up lp, yo and pull through 2 lps, yo and pull through all 3 lps on hook.

Inc: 3 dc in st indicated.

Ch 200.

Row 1 (rs): 2 dc in 4th ch from hook, dc in next 6 chs, dec over next 3 chs, * dc in next 8 chs, inc in next ch, dc in next 8 chs, dec over next 3 chs; rep from * across, dc in next 6 chs, 2 dc in last ch.

Row 2: Ch 3 [counts as first dc throughout], turn; dc in same dc and in next 6 dc, dec over next 3 sts, * dc in next 8 dc, inc in next dc, dc in next 8 dc, dec over next 3 sts; rep from * across, dc in next 6 sts, 2 dc in last dc.

Rows 3–84: Rep row 2, 82 times; fasten off after last row.

Fringe
Ridge: With rs facing, join yarn at end of row 12 with sl st; ch 1, sl st in ea st across; fasten off.

Rep along every 12th row except top edge.

For ea tassel, referring to page 143 of General Directions, cut 2 (8") lengths of yarn. Knot 1 tassel in every st along ridges. Knot 1 tassel in every st along top and bottom edges.

Beads: Knot 1 bead on every other tassel.

Ties (Make 20.)
Ch 40; fasten off, leaving long tails.

Referring to photo and using ties, tie 5 conchos evenly spaced between bottom 2 rows of fringe with square knots.

Rep with rem ties and conchos in every other horizontal panel.

Beads: Thread beads on ea tie end; knot tie below beads; weave in tails.

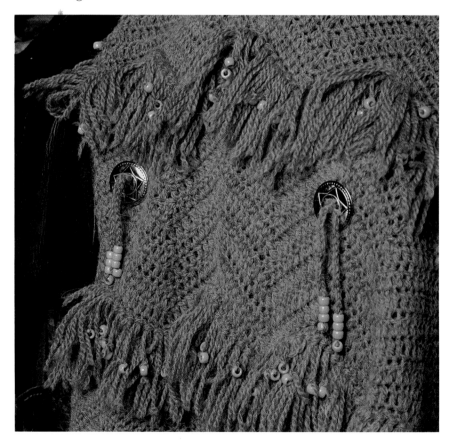

Project was stitched with Al•Pa•Ka: Camel #124.

Pinto Pony

You don't have to change colors every few stitches to create different patterns—let variegated yarn do the work for you. Then trim the afghan with colorful pony beads from your local crafts store.

Materials
Worsted-weight cotton yarn, approximately:
20 oz. (945 yd.) black, MC
10 oz. (475 yd.) red, A
12 oz. (570 yd.) black-and-white variegated, B
Sizes F and G crochet hooks or sizes to obtain gauge
6-mm pony beads:
64 black
64 red
32 white
Yarn needle

Finished Size
Approximately 40" x 40"

Gauge
With larger hook, 16 dc and 9 rows = 4"

Note: To change colors, work last yo of prev st with new color, dropping prev color to ws of work. Do not carry yarn across row.

With larger hook and A, ch 153.
Row 1 (rs): Sc in 2nd ch from hook and in ea ch across: 152 sc.
Row 2: Ch 1, turn; sc in ea sc across, change to B; fasten off A.
Rows 3–7: With B, ch 3 [counts as first dc throughout], turn; dc in next st and in ea st across: 152 dc.
Row 8: Ch 3, turn; dc in next st and in ea st across, change to A; fasten off B.

Row 9: With A, ch 1, turn; sc in first st and in ea st across.
Row 10: Ch 1, turn; sc in ea st across, change to MC; fasten off A.
Rows 11–17: With MC, ch 3, turn; dc in next st and in ea st across.
Row 18: Ch 3, turn; dc in next st and in ea st across, change to A; fasten off MC.
Row 19: Rep row 9.
Row 20: Ch 1, turn; sc in ea st across, change to B; do not fasten off A.
Row 21 (rs): Ch 3, turn; dc in next st and in ea st across; fasten off B.
Row 22 (rs): With rs facing, insert hook in top of beg ch-3, pick up A, yo and pull up lp, ch 1, sc in same st and in ea st across.
Row 23 (ws): Rep row 10.
Rows 24–32: Rep rows 11–19.
Rows 33–103: Rep rows 2–32 twice, then rep rows 2–10 once; do not change colors after last row; fasten off.

Left Edging
Row 1 (rs): With rs facing and smaller hook, join A in top left corner with sl st; ch 1, sc in same st as joining, sc evenly across left edge of afghan.
Row 2: Ch 3, turn; dc in next sc and in ea sc across.
Row 3: Ch 1, turn; sc in first dc and in ea dc across; fasten off.

Right Edging
Row 1 (rs): With rs facing and smaller hook, join A in bottom right corner with sl st; ch 1, sc in same st as joining, sc evenly across left edge of afghan.
Rows 2 and 3: Work as for rows 2 and 3 of Left Edging.

Embroidery
With rs facing and MC, work diagonal whipstitch around afghan; reverse diagonal whipstitch around afghan to form cross-stitch.

Ties (Make 16.)
With larger hook and MC, ch 36, leaving long tails at ea end; fasten off.

With rs facing, knot 1 tie at ea corner. Knot 1 tie along left edge at midpoint of ea black section. Rep along right edge.

Thread beads on ea tie end in foll sequence: 1 red, 1 black, 1 white, 1 black, and 1 red. Knot tie below beads; weave in tails.

Project was stitched with Kitchen Cotton: Black #153, Poppy Red #112, and Salt & Pepper #201.

Flower Fresh

Make bright granny squares and then join them in rippling panels for a garden of color. Measure out a few motifs and add color to your kitchen window with the matching valance on page 76.

Afghan

Materials
Worsted-weight cotton yarn, approximately:
40 oz. (1,890 yd.) white, MC
15 oz. (710 yd.) red, A
15 oz. (710 yd.) yellow, B
10 oz. (475 yd.) green, C
Size G crochet hook or size to obtain gauge
Yarn needle

Finished Size
Approximately 48" x 56"

Gauge
Flower = 2½"

Flower (Make 54 ea of A and B.)
Ch 3, join with sl st to form ring.
Rnd 1 (rs): Ch 3 [counts as first dc throughout], 2 dc in ring, (ch 3, 3 dc in ring) 3 times, ch 3; join with sl st to top of beg ch-3.
Note: Mark last rnd as rs.
Rnd 2: Sl st in next 2 dc, sl st in next ch-3 sp, ch 3, (2 dc, ch 3, 3 dc) in next ch-3 sp, * ch 1, (3 dc, ch 3, 3 dc) in next ch-3 sp; rep from * around, ch 1; join with sl st to top of beg ch-3; fasten off.

Half Flower (Make 4 ea of A and B.)
Ch 3, join with sl st to form ring.

Row 1 (ws): Ch 5, (3 dc, ch 3, 3 dc, ch 1, tr) in ring.
Row 2 (rs): Ch 5, turn; 3 dc in first ch-1 sp, ch 1, (3 dc, ch 3, 3 dc) in next ch-3 sp, ch 1, (3 dc, ch 1, tr) in next ch-5 sp; fasten off.
Note: Mark last row as rs.

Whole Strip (Make 2 beg with Flower A; make 2 beg with Flower B.)
Note: Alternate Flower colors.
Row 1 (rs): With rs facing, join MC to first Flower in corner ch-3 sp with sl st, ch 3, dc in same ch-3 sp, * ch 1, 3 dc in next ch-1 sp, ch 1, (3 dc, ch 3, 3 dc) in next ch-3 sp, ch 1, 3 dc in next ch-1 sp, ch 1, dc in next ch-3 sp **; yo, insert hook in same sp and pull up lp, insert hook in ch-3 sp of next Flower, yo and pull up lp, yo and pull through all 4 lps on hook [joining made]; dc in same ch-3 sp of next Flower; rep from * 12 times, then rep from * to ** once, dc in same ch-3 sp: 14 Flowers.
Note: Mark last row as rs.
Rows 2–4: Ch 4 [counts as first dc plus ch 1 throughout], turn; 2 dc in first ch-1 sp, ch 1, * 3 dc in next ch-1 sp, ch 1, (3 dc, ch 3, 3 dc) in next ch-3 sp, ch 1, 3 dc in next ch-1 sp, ch 1 **; yo, insert hook in next ch-1 sp and pull up lp, yo and pull through 2 lps, yo, insert hook in center of joining and pull up lp, yo and pull through 2 lps, yo insert hook in next ch-1 sp and pull up lp, yo and pull through 2

lps, yo and pull through all 4 lps on hook [dec made], ch 1; rep from * across, ending last rep at **, dc in next ch-1 sp, yo, insert hook in same ch-1 sp and pull up lp, yo and pull through 2 lps, yo, insert hook in top of beg dc, yo and pull up lp, yo and pull through all 3 lps on hook; fasten off after last row.
Rows 5–8: Rep rows 1–4 along bottom edge, changing to C in last st of last row.
Row 9: With C, rep row 2 once; fasten off.

Half Strip (Make 2 beg with Half Flower A; make 2 beg with Half Flower B.)
Note: Alternate Flower colors.
Row 1 (rs): With rs facing, join MC to first Half Flower in corner ch-5 sp with sl st; ch 4, 3 dc in same ch-3 sp, * ch 1, 3 dc in next ch-1 sp, ch 1, dc in next corner ch-3 sp **; yo, insert hook in same sp and pull up lp, insert hook in ch-3 sp of next Flower, yo and pull up lp, yo and pull through all 4 lps on hook [joining made]; dc in same ch-3 sp of next Flower, ch 1, 3 dc in next ch-1 sp, ch 1, (3 dc, ch 3, 3 dc) in next ch-3 sp; rep from * 12 times, then rep from * to ** once; yo, insert hook in same sp and pull up lp, insert hook in ch-3 sp of next Half Flower, yo and pull up lp, yo and pull through all 4 lps on hook

(continued)

Project was stitched with Kitchen Cotton: White #100, Poppy Red #112, Sunflower #157, and Forest Green #131.

[joining made]; dc in same ch-3 sp, (ch 1, 3 dc in next ch-1 sp) twice, ch 1, tr in same ch-1 sp: 13 Flowers and 2 Half Flowers.
Note: Mark last row as rs.

Rows 2–4: Ch 4 [counts as first dc plus ch 1 throughout], turn; 3 dc in first ch-1 sp, ch 1, * 3 dc in next ch-1 sp, ch 1; yo, insert hook in next ch-1 sp and pull up lp, yo and pull through 2 lps, yo, insert hook in center of joining and pull up lp, yo and pull through 2 lps, yo insert hook in next ch-1 sp and pull up lp, yo and pull through 2 lps, yo and pull through all 4 lps on hook [dec made], ch 1, 3 dc in next ch-1 sp, ch 1 **, (3 dc, ch 3, 3 dc) in next ch-3 sp, ch 1; rep from * across, ending last rep at **, (3 dc, ch 1, dc) in last ch-4 sp; fasten off after last row.

Rows 5–8: Rep rows 1–4 along bottom edge, changing to C in last st of last row.

Row 9: With C, rep row 2 once; fasten off.

Assembly
Alternating colors, whipstitch Strips and Half Strips tog.

Border
With rs facing, join C in bottom right corner with sl st; ch 1, 2 sc in same corner, sc evenly across ends of Strips to next corner, 3 sc in corner, (sc in ea sc across to next ch-3 sp, 5 sc in ch-3 sp) across to next corner, 3 sc in corner, sc evenly across ends of Strips to next corner, 2 sc in corner; join with sl st in same corner; fasten off.

Stems
With rs facing, join C in point below 1 Flower with sl st; working vertically, sl st in next 4 ch-sps [to base of Flower]; fasten off.
　　Rep for ea Stem.

Valance

Materials (for 2 valances)
Worsted-weight cotton yarn, approximately:
5 oz. (240 yd.) white, MC
5 oz. (240 yd.) red, A
5 oz. (240 yd.) yellow, B
5 oz. (240 yd.) green, C
Size G crochet hook or size to obtain gauge
Yarn needle

Finished Size
Approximately 8" x 24"

Flowers (Make 4 with A and 3 with B.)
Work same as Afghan.

Strip
Work same as Afghan.

Border
With rs facing, join C in bottom right corner with sl st; ch 1, 2 sc in same corner, sc evenly across end of Valance to next corner, 3 sc in corner, * sc in ea sc across to next ch-3 sp, (sc, ch 10, sc) in ch-3 sp; rep from * across to next corner, 3 sc in corner, sc evenly across ends of Strips to next corner, 2 sc in corner; join with sl st in same corner; fasten off.

Stems
Work same as Afghan.

Project was stitched with Kitchen Cotton: White #100, Poppy Red #112, Sunflower #157, and Forest Green #131.

Cabled Sampler

Crochet blocks of popcorns, clusters, and basket weave stitches in a variety of colors and then join them with fat cabled strips.

Afghan

Materials
Worsted weight wool-blend
  yarn, approximately:
24 oz. (1,580 yd.) gray, MC
9 oz. (595 yd.) green, A
6 oz. (395 yd.) rose, B
6 oz. (395 yd.) blue, C
Size J crochet hook or size to
  obtain gauge
Yarn needle

Finished Size
Approximately 41" x 53"

Gauge
Bobble Block = 8" x 9"
Popcorn Block = 8" x 8"
Basket Weave Block = 8" x 9"
Cable Strip = 8" wide

Pattern Stitches
Bobble: 4 sc in st indicated, drop lp from hook, insert hook in first sc of 4-sc grp, pull dropped lp through.

Popcorn: 4 dc in st indicated, drop lp from hook, insert hook in first dc of 4-dc grp, pull dropped lp through.

Front Post dc (FPdc): Yo, insert hook from front to back around post of st indicated, yo and pull up lp, (yo and pull through 2 lps) twice; sk st behind FPdc.

Back Post dc (BPdc): Yo, insert hook from back to front around post of st indicated, yo and pull up lp, (yo and pull through 2 lps) twice; sk st behind BPdc.

Front Post tr (FPtr): Yo twice, insert hook from front to back around post of next st, yo and pull up lp, (yo and pull through 2 lps) 3 times; sk st behind FPtr.

Cluster (cl): * Yo twice, insert hook in st indicated, yo and pull up lp, (yo and pull through 2 lps) twice; rep from * 3 times, yo and pull through all 5 lps on hook.

Bobble Block (Make 2 ea with MC and C; make 1 ea with A and B.)
Ch 34.
Row 1 (ws): Sc in 2nd ch from hook and in ea ch across: 33 sc.
Row 2 (rs): Ch 1, turn; sc in first sc, * ch 1, sk next sc, bobble in next sc, ch 1, sk next sc, sc in next sc; rep from * across: 8 bobbles.
Note: Mark last row as rs.
Row 3: Ch 2, turn; sc in first ch-1 sp, * ch 1, sc in next ch-1 sp; rep from * across to last sc, ch 1, sc in last sc: 17 ch-1 sps.
Row 4: Ch 2, turn; bobble in first ch-1 sp, ch 1, sc in next ch-1 sp, * ch 1, bobble in next ch-1 sp,

ch 1, sc in next ch-1 sp; rep from * across to last sc, sc in last sc: 8 bobbles.
Row 5: Rep row 3.
Row 6: Ch 1, turn; sc in first sc, ch 1, bobble in next ch-1 sp, ch 1, * sc in next ch-1 sp, ch 1, bobble in next ch-1 sp, ch 1; rep from * across to last sc, sc in last sc: 8 bobbles.
Rows 7–33: Rep rows 3–6, 6 times, then rep rows 3–5 once; do not fasten off.

Edging
Ch 1, turn; sc in ea sc across to corner, 3 sc in corner, * sc evenly across to next corner, 3 sc in next corner; rep from * around; join with sl st to beg sc; fasten off.

Popcorn Block (Make 4 with B; make 1 ea with MC and C.)
Ch 4, join with sl st to form ring.
Rnd 1 (rs): Ch 3, 3 dc in ring, drop lp from hook, insert hook in

---

Project was stitched with Wool-Ease: Slate Heather #108, Green Heather #130, Tapestry Heather #141, and Blue Mist #115.

top of beg ch-3, pull dropped lp through [beg popcorn made], ch 4, (popcorn, ch 4) 3 times; join with sl st to top of beg popcorn: 4 popcorns.

Note: Mark last rnd as rs.

Rnd 2: Sl st in first ch-4 sp, ch 3, (2 dc, ch 3, 3 dc) in same ch-4 sp, * (3 dc, ch 3, 3 dc) in next ch-4 sp; rep from * around; join with sl st to top of beg ch-3.

Rnd 3: Sl st in next 2 dc, sl st in next ch-4 sp, ch 3, (2 dc, ch 3, 3 dc) in same ch-4 sp, * sk 2 dc, 3 dc between next 2 dc **, (3 dc, ch 3, 3 dc) in next ch-4 sp; rep from * around, ending last rep at **; join with sl st to top of beg ch-3.

Rnd 4: Sl st in next 2 dc, sl st in next ch-4 sp, ch 3, (2 dc, ch 3, 3 dc) in same ch-4 sp, * ch 1, sk next 2 dc, popcorn between next 2 dc, ch 1, popcorn in center dc of next 3-dc grp, ch 1, popcorn between next 2 dc, ch 2 **, (3 dc, ch 3, 3 dc) in next corner ch-4 sp; rep from * around, ending last rep at **; join with sl st to top of beg ch-3.

Rnd 5: Sl st in next 2 dc, sl st in next ch-4 sp, ch 3, (2 dc, ch 3, 3 dc) in same ch-4 sp, * (ch 1, popcorn in next ch-1 sp) 4 times, ch 2 **, (3 dc, ch 3, 3 dc) in next corner ch-4 sp; rep from * around, ending last rep at **; join with sl st to top of beg ch-3.

Rnd 6: Sl st in next 2 dc, sl st in next ch-4 sp, ch 3, (2 dc, ch 3, 3 dc) in same ch-4 sp, * (ch 1, popcorn in next ch-1 sp) 5 times, ch 2 **, (3 dc, ch 3, 3 dc) in next corner ch-4 sp; rep from * around, ending last rep at **; join with sl st to top of beg ch-3.

Rnd 7: Sl st in next 2 dc, sl st in next ch-4 sp, ch 3, (2 dc, ch 3, 3 dc) in same ch-4 sp, * (ch 1, popcorn in next ch-1 sp) 6 times, ch 2 **, (3 dc, ch 3, 3 dc) in next

corner ch-4 sp; rep from * around, ending last rep at **; join with sl st to top of beg ch-3.

Rnd 8: Ch 3, dc in next 2 dc, * (3 dc, ch 3, 3 dc) in next corner ch-4 sp, dc in ea st and sp across to next corner ch-4 sp; rep from * around; join with sl st to beg ch-3; fasten off.

Basket Weave Block (Make 4 with A; make 1 ea with MC and C.)

Ch 32.

Row 1 (ws): Dc in 4th ch from hook and in ea ch across: 30 dc.

Rows 2–5: Ch 3 [counts as dc throughout], turn; sk first dc, * FPdc around next 4 dc, BPdc around next 4 dc; rep from * across, dc in top of tch.

Rows 6–9: Ch 3, turn; sk first dc, * BPdc around next 4 dc, FPdc around next 4 dc; rep from * across, dc in top of tch.

Rows 10–21: Rep rows 2–9 once, then rep rows 2–5 once; do not fasten off.

Edging

Ch 1, turn; sc in ea sc across to corner, 3 sc in corner, * sc evenly across to next corner, 3 sc in next corner; rep from * around; join with sl st to beg sc; fasten off.

Cable Strip (Make 2.)

With MC, ch 32.

Row 1 (ws): Dc in 4th ch from hook and in ea ch across: 30 dc.

Row 2 (rs): Ch 3 [counts as first dc throughout], turn; dc in next st, BPdc around next 2 sts, * FPdc around next st, BPdc around next 2 sts; sk 2 sts, FPtr around next 2 sts, working in front of last 2 sts, FPtr around 2 sk sts [cable made]; BPdc around next 2 sts, FPdc around next st, BPdc around next 2 sts; rep from * once, dc in last 2 dc.

Note: Mark last row as rs.

Row 3: Ch 3, turn; dc in next dc, FPdc around next 2 sts, * BPdc around next st, FPdc around next 2 sts, BPdc around next 4 sts, FPdc around next 2 sts, BPdc around next st, FPdc around next 2 sts; rep from * once, dc in last 2 dc.

Rep rows 2 and 3 alternately until piece measures approximately 52"; fasten off after last row.

Assembly

Referring to *Placement Diagram,* whipstitch blocks tog in strips.

Whipstitch block strips and cable strips tog.

Border

Rnd 1 (rs): With rs facing, join MC in any corner with sl st, ch 1, sc in same st as joining, sc evenly across to next corner, * 3 sc in corner, sc evenly across to next corner; rep from * around; join with sl st to beg sc.

Rnd 2: Ch 1, sc in next sc, ch 3, sk next sc, cl in next sc, ch 3, sk next sc, * sc in next sc, ch 3, sk next sc, cl in next sc, ch 3, sk next sc; rep from * around; join with sl st to beg sc; fasten off.

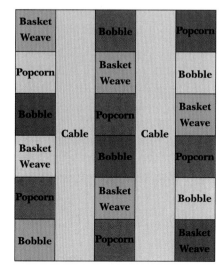

Placement Diagram

Popcorn Star

Busy moms like me are always looking for shortcuts for cooking, cleaning, and even crocheting! These oversize blocks work up quickly.

Materials
Chunky-weight brushed acrylic yarn, approximately:
54 oz. (2,430 yd.) rose
Size J crochet hook or size to obtain gauge
Yarn needle

Finished Size
Approximately 50" x 61"

Gauge
Ea Square = 11¼"

Pattern Stitches
Popcorn: 5 dc in st indicated, drop lp from hook, insert hook in first dc of 5-dc grp, pull dropped lp through.

V-st: (Dc, ch 2, dc) in st or sp indicated.

Cl: (Yo, insert hook in st indicated, yo and pull through 2 lps) twice, yo and pull through all 3 lps on hook.

Square (Make 20.)
Ch 6, join with sl st to form ring.

Rnd 1 (rs): Ch 3 [counts as first dc throughout], 27 dc in ring; join with sl st to top of beg ch-3: 28 dc.
Note: Mark last rnd as rs.

Rnd 2: Ch 3, dc in next 6 dc, * ch 2, dc in next 7 dc; rep from * around; join with sl st to top of beg ch-3.

Rnd 3: Ch 3, dc in next 6 dc, (2 dc, ch 2, 2 dc) in next ch-2 sp, * dc in next 7 dc, (2 dc, ch 2, 2 dc) in next ch-2 sp; rep from * around; join with sl st to top of beg ch-3: 44 dc.

Rnd 4: Ch 3, dc in next 6 dc, * popcorn in next dc, dc in next dc, (2 dc, ch 2, 2 dc) in next ch-2 sp, dc in next dc, popcorn in next dc **, dc in next 7 dc; rep from * around, ending last rep at **; join with sl st to top of beg ch-3.

Rnd 5: Sl st in next dc, ch 3, dc in next 4 dc, * popcorn in next dc, dc in top of next popcorn, dc in next 3 dc, (2 dc, ch 2, 2 dc) in next ch-2 sp, dc in next 3 dc, dc in top of next popcorn, popcorn in next dc **, dc in next 5 dc; rep from * around, ending last rep at **; join with sl st to top of beg ch-3.

Rnd 6: Sl st in next dc, ch 3, dc in next 2 dc, * popcorn in next dc, dc in top of next popcorn, dc in next 6 dc, (2 dc, ch 2, 2 dc) in next ch-2 sp, dc in next 6 dc, dc in top of next popcorn, popcorn in next dc **, dc in next 3 dc; rep from * around, ending last rep at **; join with sl st to top of beg ch-3.

Rnd 7: Ch 3, 4 dc in same st, drop lp from hook, insert hook in 3rd ch of beg ch-3 and pull dropped lp through [beg popcorn made], * dc in next dc, popcorn in next dc, dc in top of next popcorn, dc in next 9 dc, 3 dc in next ch-2 sp, dc in next 9 dc, dc in top of next popcorn **, popcorn in next dc; rep from * around, ending at **; join with sl st to top of beg popcorn.

Rnd 8: Sl st in next dc, ch 3, beg popcorn in same st, * dc in top of next popcorn, dc in next 11 dc, 3 dc in next dc, dc in next 11 dc, dc in top of next popcorn **, popcorn in next dc; rep from * around, ending last rep at **; join with sl st to top of beg popcorn; fasten off.

Assembly
Afghan is 5 squares long and 4 squares wide. Whipstitch squares tog.

Border
Rnd 1 (rs): With rs facing, join yarn with sl st in any corner, ch 5, (dc, ch 3, V-st) in same st, (sk next 2 sts, V-st in next st) across to next corner, * (V-st, ch 3, V-st) in corner sp, (sk next 2 sts, V-st in next st) across to next corner; rep from * around; join with sl st to 3rd ch of beg ch-5.

Rnd 2: Ch 3, dc in next dc, ch 3, (dc, ch 3) twice in corner ch-3 sp, (cl in next dc, ch 3) across to next corner, * (dc, ch 3) twice in corner ch-3 sp, (cl in next dc, ch 3) across to next corner; rep from * around; join with sl st to top of beg ch-3.

Rnd 3: Sl st in first ch-3 sp, ch 1, (sc, ch 1) twice in same ch-3 sp, * (sc, ch 1) 3 times in corner ch-3 sp, (sc, ch 1) twice in ea ch-3 sp across to corner; rep from * around; join with sl st to beg sl st.

Rnd 4: Sl st in first ch-1 sp, ch 1, sc in same sp, ch 1, (sc, ch 1) in next ch-1 sp and in ea ch-1 sp around; join with sl st to beg sl st; fasten off.

Project was stitched with Jiffy: Dusty Rose #141.

Rex the Cat

Cat-lovers will go for this feisty feline. His striped coat is stitched in frosted yarn, and the red background is sprinkled with fun flecks of additional color.

Materials
Worsted-weight wool-blend yarn, approximately:
18 oz. (1,185 yd.) red, MC
7½ oz. (490 yd.) white, A
10 oz. (650 yd.) black, B
Size J crochet hook or size to obtain gauge

Finished Size
Approximately 41" x 53"

Gauge
14 sc and 16 rows = 4"

Note: To change colors, work last yo of prev st with new color, dropping prev color to ws of work. Do not carry yarn across row.

With MC, ch 133.
Row 1 (rs): Sc in 2nd ch from hook and in ea ch across: 132 sc.
Rows 2–16: Ch 1, turn; sc in ea sc across.

Row 17: Ch 1, turn; reading *Chart* on pages 84 and 85 from right to left, sc in first 89 sc, change to A, sc in next 3 sc, (change to B, sc in next sc, change to A, sc in next 2 sc) twice, change to B, sc in next sc, change to A, sc in next 5 sc, change to B, sc in next 7 sc, change to A, sc in next 6 sc, change to B, sc in next 5 sc, change to MC, sc in ea sc across.
Row 18: Ch 1, turn; reading *Chart* from left to right, sc in first 9 sc, change to B, sc in next 6 sc, change to A, sc in next 7 sc, change to B, sc in next 7 sc, change to A, sc in next 4 sc, (change to B, sc in next sc, change to A, sc in next 2 sc) twice, change to B, sc in next sc, change to A, sc in next 3 sc, change to B, sc in next sc, change to A, sc in next 2 sc, change to B, sc in next sc, change to MC, sc in ea sc across.
Rows 19–200: Cont foll *Chart* as est, reading odd (rs) rows from right to left and even (ws) rows from left to right; do not fasten off.

Border
Rnd 1 (ws): Ch 1, * sc evenly across to corner, 3 sc in corner; rep from * around; join with sl st to beg sc; fasten off.
Rnd 2: With rs facing, join B to top right corner with sl st; sc in same st and ea st across to corner, * 3 sc in corner, sc in ea st across to corner; rep from * around; join with sl st to beg sc.
Rnds 3–7: Ch 1, sc in ea st across to corner, * 3 sc in corner, sc in ea st across to corner; rep from * around; join with sl st to beg sc; fasten off after last rnd.

(continued)

Chart Key
■ **Red**
□ **White**
▧ **Black**

Each square on the chart represents one single crochet stitch. Because the work is turned after each row, be sure to read all right side rows from right to left and all wrong side rows from left to right.

Project was stitched with Wool-Ease: Red Sprinkles #112, White Frost #501, and Black Frost #502.

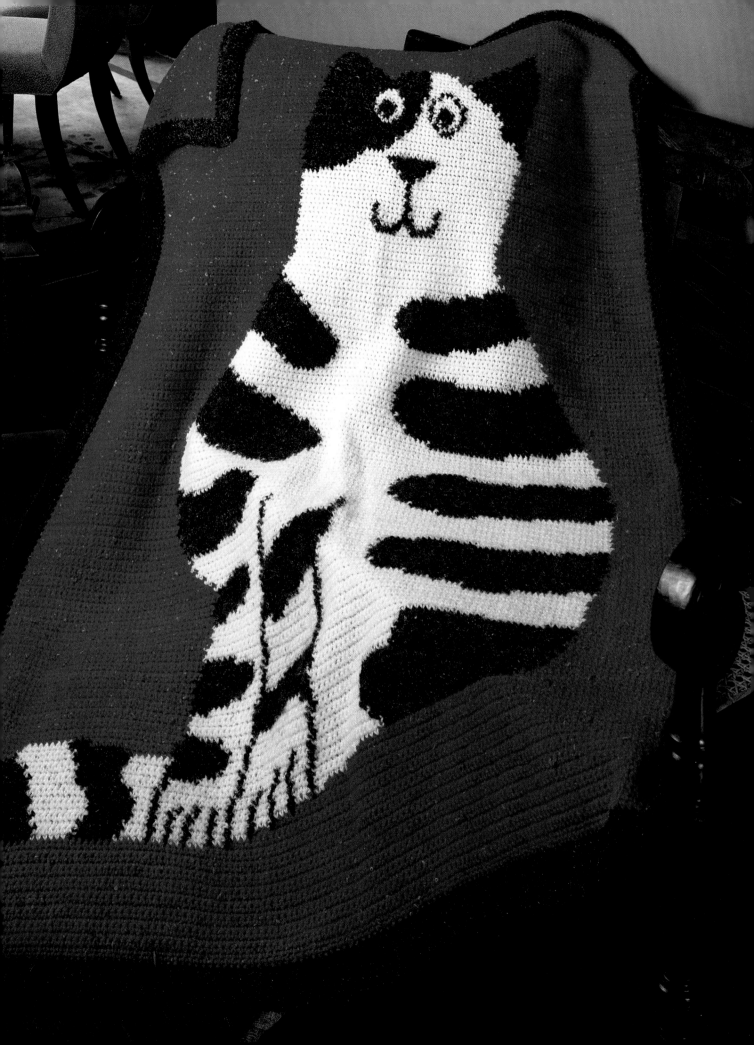

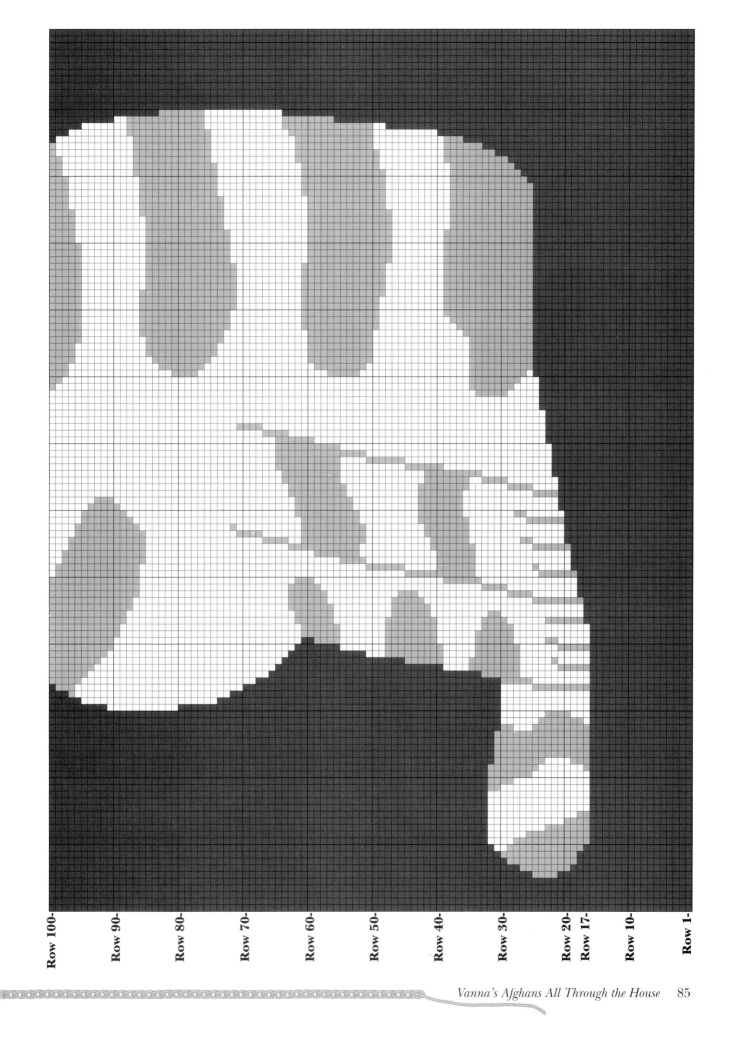

Play Ball!

Nicholas loves baseball, and this bright afghan captures the spirit of America's favorite pastime. The matching pillow makes a great cushion to use while watching the big game on television.

Afghan

Materials
Worsted-weight acrylic yarn, approximately:
30 oz. (1,500 yd.) blue, MC
12 oz. (600 yd.) white, A
12 oz. (600 yd.) red, B
Sizes G and H crochet hooks or sizes to obtain gauge
Yarn needle

Finished Size
Approximately 46" x 60"

Gauge
With larger hook, 7 dc and 4 rows = 2"

Center
With larger hook and MC, ch 157.
Row 1 (rs): Dc in 4th ch from hook and in next 5 chs, (ch 1, sk 1 ch, dc in next 6 chs) across to last ch, dc in last ch: 134 dc.
Rows 2–60: Ch 3 [counts as dc throughout], turn; sk first dc, (dc in next 6 dc, ch 1, sk next ch-1 sp) across to last 7 dc, dc in last 7 dc, changing to B in last st of last row.

Top Border
Row 1 (rs): With B, ch 1, turn; sc in first st, sc in ea st and ch-1 sp across: 155 sc.
Rows 2–4: Ch 1, turn; sc in ea st

across, changing to A in last st of last row.
Row 5: With A, ch 3, turn; sk first 2 sc, (dc in next 6 sc, ch 1, sk 1 sc) across to last 7 sc, dc in last 7 sc: 134 dc.
Rows 6–16: Ch 3, turn; sk first dc, (dc in next 6 dc, ch 1, sk next ch-1 sp) across to last 7 dc, dc in last 7 dc; fasten off after last row.

Bottom Border
Row 1 (rs): With rs facing, join B in bottom left corner with sl st; ch 1, work 155 sc evenly sp across.
Rows 2–16: Rep rows 2–16 of Top Border.

Side Border
Row 1 (rs): With rs facing, join B to free Center corner with sl st; ch 1, working in ends of rows, work 90 sc evenly sp across.
Rows 2–4: Rep rows 2–4 of Top Border.
Row 5: With A, ch 3, turn; sk first sc, dc in next 5 sc, (sk 1 sc, dc in next 6 sc) across: 78 dc.
Rows 6–16: Ch 3, turn; dc in next 5 sc, (sk next ch-1 sp, dc in next 6 dc) across; fasten off after last row.
  Rep along rem side.

Corner
Row 1 (rs): With rs facing, join MC to bottom right corner of Top Border with sl st, ch 1, working in ends of rows, work 23 sc evenly sp across.
Rows 2–13: Ch 3, turn; dc in next dc and in ea dc across: 23 dc.

Row 14: Ch 1, turn; sc in first dc and in ea dc across; fasten off.
  Whipstitch Corner side to Side Border.
  Rep for rem 3 corners.

Edging
Rnd 1 (rs): With rs facing and smaller hook, join B to top right corner with sl st, ch 1, sc in same st and in ea st across to next corner, * 3 sc in corner, sc evenly across to next corner; rep from * around; join with sl st to beg sc.
Rnds 2–4: Ch 1, turn; sc in same st and in ea st across to next corner, * 3 sc in corner, sc in ea st across to next corner; rep from * around; join with sl st to beg sc; fasten off after last rnd.

Baseball (Make 4.)
With larger hook and A, ch 8.
Row 1 (rs): Sc in 2nd ch from hook and in ea ch across: 7 sc.
Rows 2–4: Ch 1, turn; 2 sc in first sc, sc in ea sc across to last sc, 2 sc in last sc.
Rows 5–8: Ch 1, turn; sc in first sc and in ea sc across: 13 sc.
Rows 9–11: Ch 1, turn; insert hook in first sc and pull up lp, insert hook in next sc and pull up lp, yo and pull through all 3 lps on hook [dec made], sc in ea sc across to last 2 sc, dec in last 2 sc.
Row 12: Ch 1, turn; sc in first sc and in ea sc across; fasten off: 7 sc.

(continued)

Project was stitched with Jamie 4 Ply: Blue #109, White #100, and Red #113.

Edging
Join B with sl st in any st, ch 1, sc evenly around; join with sl st to beg sc; fasten off.

Stitching
With rs facing, insert larger hook from front to back of Baseball, join B with sl st, sl st from front to back through Baseball, referring to photo for placement; fasten off.

Rep for rem stitching.

Finishing
With B, center and appliqué 1 Baseball to ea Corner.

Center Stripes
With rs facing and larger hook, join A in ch below first ch-1 sp in row 2 of center with sl st, working vertically, sl st in ea ch-1 sp to Top Border; fasten off.
Rep for ea vertical row of ch-1 sps.

Border Stripes
With rs facing and larger hook, join MC in sc below first ch-1 sp in row 5 of Top Border with sl st, working vertically, sl st in ea ch-1 sp to Edging; fasten off.
Rep for ea vertical row of ch-1 sps around.

Pillow

Materials
Worsted-weight acrylic yarn, approximately:
12 oz. (600 yd.) white, MC
6 oz. (300 yd.) red, CC
Size H crochet hook or size to obtain gauge
Polyester stuffing

Finished Size
Approximately 16"

Gauge
12 sc and 14 rows = 4"

Pillow Front
With MC, ch 23.
Row 1 (rs): Sc in 2nd ch from hook and in ea ch across: 22 sc.
Note: Mark last row as rs.
Rows 2–16: Ch 1, turn; 2 sc in first sc, sc in ea sc across to last sc, 2 sc in last sc.
Rows 17–40: Ch 1, turn; sc in first sc and in ea sc across: 52 sc.
Rows 41–55: Ch 1, turn; insert hook in first sc and pull up lp, insert hook in next sc and pull up lp, yo and pull through all 3 lps on hook [dec made], sc in ea sc across to last 2 sc, dec in last 2 sc.
Row 56: Ch 1, turn; sc in first sc and in ea sc across; fasten off: 22 sc.

Edging
Attach CC to any st with sl st, ch 1, sc evenly around; join with sl st to beg sc; fasten off.

Stitching
With rs facing, insert larger hook from front to back of Pillow Front, join MC with sl st, sl st from front to back through Pillow Front, referring to photo for placement; fasten off.
Rep for rem stitching.

Pillow Back
Work as for Pillow Front.

Assembly
With ws tog, join MC in any st with sl st, working through all lps, sc Pillow Front to Pillow Back, stuff moderately before completing sc rnd; join with sl st to beg sc; fasten off.

Project was stitched with Jamie 4 Ply: White #100 and Red #113.

Dutch Tile

Treat yourself to a traditional blue-and-white throw. Work a few embroidered cross-stitches between the granny squares.

Materials

Worsted-weight acrylic yarn, approximately:
36 oz. (1,875 yd.) blue, MC
42 oz. (2,185 yd.) white, CC
Sizes G and H crochet hooks or sizes to obtain gauge
Yarn needle

Finished Size

Approximately 53" x 62½"

Gauge

Granny Square = 2¾"
With larger hook, 8 sc and
8 rows = 2"

Granny Square A (Make 120.)

With larger hook and CC, ch 3, join with sl st to form ring.
Rnd 1 (rs): Ch 3 [counts as first dc throughout], 2 dc in ring, (ch 3, 3 dc in ring) 3 times, ch 3; join with sl st to top of beg ch-3; fasten off.
Note: Mark last rnd as rs.
Rnd 2 (rs): With rs facing, join MC in any ch-3 sp with sl st, ch 3, (2 dc, ch 3, 3 dc) in same sp, * ch 1, (3 dc, ch 3, 3 dc) in next ch-3 sp; rep from * around, ch 1; join with sl st to top of beg ch-3; fasten off.

Granny Square B (Make 100.)

With larger hook and MC, ch 3, join with sl st to form ring.
Rnd 1 (rs): Ch 3 [counts as first dc throughout], 2 dc in ring, (ch 3, 3 dc in ring) 3 times, ch 3; join with sl st to top of beg ch-3; fasten off.
Note: Mark last rnd as rs.
Rnd 2 (rs): With rs facing, join CC in any ch-3 sp with sl st, ch 3, (2 dc, ch 3, 3 dc) in same sp, * ch 1, (3 dc, ch 3, 3 dc) in next

ch-3 sp; rep from * around, ch 1; join with sl st to top of beg ch-3; fasten off.

Block Assembly

Referring to photograph, whipstitch 4 Granny Square As tog to form 1 A Block. Rep to make 30 A Blocks. Whipstitch 4 Granny Square Bs tog to form 1 B Block. Rep to make 25 B Blocks.

Strip Assembly

Referring to *Assembly Diagram,* alternate 6 A Blocks and 5 B Blocks. Whipstitch Blocks tog. Rep to make 5 Strips.
Note: To change colors, work last

yo of prev st with new color, dropping prev color to ws of work.
Row 1 (rs): With rs facing and larger hook, join MC to bottom right corner with sl st, ch 1, work 242 sc evenly sp across.
Row 2: Ch 3 [counts as first dc], turn; sk first sc, dc in next sc, * change to CC, dc in next 2 sc, change to MC, dc in next 2 sc; rep from * across.
Row 3: With MC, ch 1, turn; sc in first dc and in ea dc across; fasten off: 242 sc.
Row 4 (rs): With rs facing, join CC in bottom right corner with sl st, ch 1, sc in same sc and in ea sc across: 242 sc.

Project was stitched with Keepsake Sayelle: Royal Blue #109 and White #100.

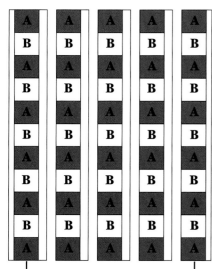

Beg Strip   *End Strip*
Assembly Diagram

Rows 5–14: Ch 1, turn; sc in first sc and in ea sc across; fasten off: 242 sc.

Rows 15–17: Rep rows 1–3 once. Rep to complete 3 Strips.

End Strip: Work rows 1–14 to complete End Strip.

Beg Strip: Work rows 1–17 along 1 side of 1 Strip.

Row 18 (rs): With rs facing and larger hook, join MC to top left corner of Beg Strip with sl st, ch 1, work 242 sc evenly sp across Beg Strip.

Rows 19 and 20: Rep rows 2 and 3 once.

Row 21 (rs): With rs facing, join CC in top left corner with sl st, ch 1, sc in same sc and in ea sc across: 242 sc.

Rows 22–31: Rep rows 5–14 once.

Embroidery

Foll *Embroidery Chart* and referring to st diagram on page 142, work cross-stitch in ea sc panel.

Assembly

Referring to *Assembly Diagram*, whipstitch Strips tog.

Border

Rnd 1 (rs): With rs facing and smaller hook, join MC to top right corner with sl st, ch 1, sc in same corner, * sc evenly across to next corner, 3 sc in corner; rep from * around; join with sl st to beg sc.

Rnd 2 (ws): Ch 3, turn; dc in same sc, change to CC, dc in same sc, dc in next sc, * change to MC, dc in next 2 sc, change to CC, dc in next 2 sc; rep from * around, working 3 dc in ea corner and maintaining color pat; join with sl st to top of tch.

Rnd 3: With MC, ch 1, turn; * sc in ea dc across to next corner, 3 sc in corner; rep from * around; join with sl st to beg sc; fasten off.

Rnd 4 (rs): With rs facing, join CC in top right corner with sl st, ch 3, * sk next sc, sl st in next sc, ch 3; rep from * around; join with sl st to beg sl st; fasten off.

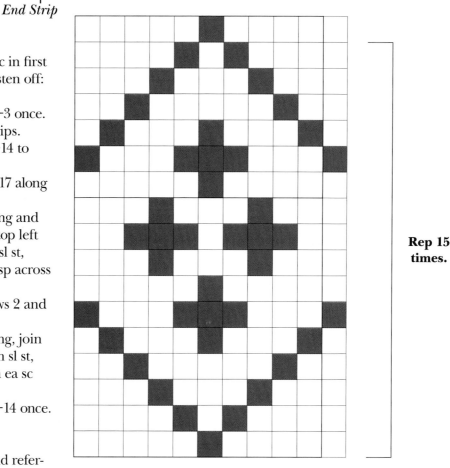

Rep 15 times.

Embroidery Chart

Purple Passion

Bring a bold color into your decor with this regal throw.
Weave crocheted cords through the border and tie
them in bows at the corners.

Materials

Worsted-weight mohair-blend
yarn, approximately:
46 oz. (4,125 yd.) purple
Sizes I and J crochet hooks or
sizes to obtain gauge
2½" square cardboard

Finished Size

Approximately 53" x 61"

Gauge

In pat with larger hook, 11 sts and
16 rows = 4"

Pattern Stitches

Front Post dc (FPdc): Yo, insert
hook from front to back around
post of st indicated, yo and pull
up lp, (yo and pull through 2 lps)
twice; sk st behind FPdc.

Back Post dc (BPdc): Yo, insert
hook from back to front around
post of st indicated, yo and pull
up lp, (yo and pull through 2 lps)
twice; sk st behind BPdc.

With larger hook, ch 135.
Row 1 (rs): Sc in 2nd ch from
hook and in ea ch across: 134 sc.
Row 2: Ch 1, turn; sc in first sc
and in ea st across.
Row 3: Ch 1, turn; sc in first sc,
(FPdc around next 4 sc on row 1,
sc in next 4 sc) across to last 5 sc,
FPdc around next 4 sc on row 1,
sc in last sc.
Row 4: Rep row 2.

Row 5: Ch 1, turn; sc in first sc,
(FPdc around next 4 FPdc, sc in
next 4 sc) across to last 5 sts, FPdc
around next 4 FPdc, sc in last sc.

Rep rows 4 and 5 alternately
until piece measures approximately 55"; do not fasten off after
last row.

Border

Rnd 1 (rs): With rs facing and
smaller hook, ch 3, dc evenly
across to next corner, * 3 dc in
corner, dc evenly across to next
corner; rep from * around, 2 dc
in corner; join with sl st to top of
beg ch-3.
Rnd 2: Ch 3, turn; * 3 dc in next
dc [corner], (FPdc around next
2 dc, BPdc around next 2 dc)
across to next corner **, 3 dc in
corner; rep from * around, ending last rep at **; join with sl st to
top of beg ch-3.
Rnds 3–8: Ch 3, turn; * BPdc
around ea FPdc and FPdc around
ea BPdc across to corner, 3 dc in
corner; rep from * around, sl st to
top of beg ch-3.
Rnd 9: Ch 1, turn; * sc in ea st
across to corner, 3 sc in corner;
rep from * around; join with sl st
to beg sc; fasten off.

Ties

With smaller hook and holding 2
strands tog, make 2 (77") chains
and 2 (85") chains.

Weave 1 (77") chain through
rnd 1 of Border along 1 short
edge. Rep with rem 77" chain
along opposite edge. Weave 85"
chains along long edges. Tie 1
bow at ea corner.

Tassels

For ea tassel, referring to page
143 of General Directions, wrap
yarn around 2½" piece of cardboard 15 times. Attach 1 tassel to
ea end of ea Tie.

Project was stitched with Imagine: Purple Haze #338.

Garden Trellis

Long double crochet stitches create a wonderful lattice pattern in two shades of green. Surprise! This intricate-looking design requires color changes only at the end of every other row.

Materials
Worsted-weight acrylic yarn, approximately:
24 oz. (1,250 yd.) dark green, MC
24 oz. (1,250 yd.) light green, CC
Size K crochet hook or size to obtain gauge

Finished Size
Approximately 46" x 59"

Gauge
In pat, 10 sts and 13 rows = 4"

Note: To change colors, work last yo of prev st with new color, dropping prev color to ws of work. Do not carry yarn across row.

Pattern Stitch
Long dc (Ldc): Yo, insert hook in sp indicated, pull up ¾" lp, (yo and draw through 2 lps) twice.

With CC, ch 112, drop CC, pick up MC, yo and pull through lp on hook [color change ch made], with MC, ch 1: 114 chs.
Row 1 (rs): With MC, sc in 2nd ch from hook and in ea ch across: 113 sc.
Row 2: Ch 1, turn; sc in ea st across, change to CC in last st.
Row 3: With CC, ch 1, turn; sc in first sc, * sk next sc, Ldc in next st 3 rows below [foundation ch], sc in next sc, Ldc in same st as prev Ldc [V made], sk next sc [behind Ldc], sc in next sc; rep from * across: 113 sts [28 Vs].
Row 4: Ch 1, turn; sc in ea st across, change to MC in last st: 113 sc.
Row 5: With MC, ch 1, turn; sc in first 2 sc, * Ldc in next st 3 rows below [center of V], sk sc behind Ldc, sc in next 3 sc; rep from * across to last 3 sts, Ldc in next st 3 rows below, sk sc behind Ldc, sc in last 2 sc: 113 sts [28 Ldc].
Row 6: Rep row 2.
Row 7: With CC, ch 1, turn; sc in first 3 sc, * sk next sc, Ldc in next st 3 rows below, sc in next sc, Ldc in same st as prev Ldc [V made], sk next sc [behind Ldc], sc in next sc; rep from * across to last 2 sc, sc in last 2 sc: 113 sts [27 Vs].
Row 8: Rep row 4.

Row 9: With MC, ch 1, turn; sc in first 4 sc, * Ldc in next st 3 rows below [center of V], sk sc behind Ldc, sc in next 3 sc; rep from * across to last st, sc in last sc: 113 sts [27 Ldc].
Row 10: Rep row 2.
Row 11: With CC, ch 1, turn; sc in first sc, * sk next sc, Ldc in next st 3 rows below, sc in next sc, Ldc in same st as prev Ldc [V made], sk next sc [behind Ldc], sc in next sc; rep from * across: 113 sts [28 Vs].
Rows 12–191: Rep rows 4–11, 22 times, then rep rows 4–7 once; do not fasten off.

Border
Rnd 1 (rs): With rs facing, 2 sc in last st, work 147 sc evenly sp across to next corner, 3 sc in corner, sc in free lp of ea foundation ch, 3 sc in corner, work 147 sc evenly sp across to next corner, 2 sc in corner; join with sl st to beg sc of row 191; fasten off.
Rnd 2: With rs facing, join MC in same corner with sl st, sl st in first 2 sc, * (sl st, ch 3, sl st) in next sc, sl st in next 2 sc; rep from * around, (sl st, ch 3, sl st) in last st; join with sl st to beg sl st; fasten off.

Be sure to work loosely and count, count, count!

Project was stitched with Keepsake Sayelle: Sage #132 and Pine #182.

Vertical Ripple

Turn a traditional design sideways for a fresh look. Long chenille fringe accents the change in direction.

Materials
Worsted-weight chenille yarn, approximately:
19¾ oz. (1,220 yd.) variegated blue, MC
11¼ oz. (700 yd.) cream, CC
Size H crochet hook or size to obtain gauge

Finished Size
Approximately 43" x 53", without fringe

Gauge
In pat, 16 sts and 9 rows = 4"

Pattern Stitches
Beg dec: (Yo, insert hook in next st, yo and pull up lp, yo and pull through 2 lps) twice, yo and pull through all 3 lps on hook.
Dec: (Yo, insert hook in next st, yo and pull up lp, yo and pull through 2 lps) 5 times, yo and pull through all 6 lps on hook.
Inc: 5 dc in st indicated.

With MC, ch 213.
Row 1 (rs): Beg dec in 3rd ch from hook, dc in next 5 chs, inc in next ch, dc in next 5 chs, * dec in next ch, dc in next 5 chs, inc in next ch, dc in next 5 chs; rep from * across to last 2 chs, beg dec in last 2 chs: 213 sts.
Row 2: Ch 1, turn; sk first st, sc in next st and in ea st across to tch, sk tch: 211 sc.
Row 3: Ch 3, turn; sk first sc, beg dec in next sc, dc in next 5 sc, inc in next sc, dc in next 5 sc, * dec in next sc, dc in next 5 sc, inc in next sc, dc in next 5 sc; rep from * across to last 2 sc, beg dc in last 2 sc: 213 sts.
Rows 4 and 5: Rep rows 2 and 3.
Row 6: Ch 1, turn; sk first st, sc in next st and in ea st across to tch, change to CC, sk tch: 211 sc.
Row 7: With CC, ch 3, turn; sk first sc, beg dec in next sc, * (ch 1, sk next sc, dc in next dc) twice, ch 1, sk next sc, inc in next sc, (ch 1, sk next sc, dc in next sc) twice, ch 1, sk next sc **, dec in next sc; rep from * across, ending last rep at **, beg dec in last 2 sc.
Row 8: Rep row 2.
Row 9: Rep row 7, changing to MC in last st.
Rows 10 and 11: Rep rows 2 and 3.
Rows 12–96: Rep rows 2–11, 8 times, then rep rows 2–6 once.

Fringe
For ea tassel, referring to page 143 of General Directions, cut 5 (14") lengths of yarn. Working in ends of rows and matching colors, knot 2 MC tassels in ea MC band and 1 CC tassel in ea CC band.

Project was stitched with Chenille Sensations: Venice Print #408 and Antique White #98.

Aran Fisherman

This crocheted version of a knitted classic will challenge experienced crocheters with lots of crossed post stitches. The rope and cable stitches represent the traditional rigging of Irish fishing boats.

Materials
Worsted-weight mohair-blend yarn, approximately:
52½ oz. (4,665 yd.) ecru
Size I crochet hook or size to obtain gauge

Finished Size
Approximately 51" x 66"

Gauge
In pat, 13 sts and 16 rows = 4"

Pattern Stitches
Front Post dc (FPdc): Yo, insert hook from front to back around post of st indicated, yo and pull up lp, (yo and pull through 2 lps) twice; sk st behind FPdc.

Front Post tr (FPtr): Yo twice, insert hook from front to back around post of next st, yo and pull up lp, (yo and pull through 2 lps) 3 times; sk st behind FPtr.

Front cable: Sk 3 sts, FPtr around next 2 post sts; working behind last 2 sts, sc in 3rd sk st; working in front of last 3 sts, FPtr around first 2 sk sts.

Back cable: Sk 3 sts, FPtr around next 2 sts; working behind last 2 sts, sc in 3rd sk st; working behind last 2 Fptr, FPtr around first 2 sk sts.

Cable Strip (Make 2.)
Ch 34.
Row 1 (rs): Sc in 2nd ch from hook and in ea ch across: 33 sc.
Note: Mark last row as rs.
Row 2 and all Even-Numbered Rows (ws): Ch 1, turn; sc in ea st across.
Row 3: Sc in first 2 sc, (FPdc around next 2 sc on row 1, sc in next sc, FPdc around next 2 sc on row 1, sc in next 3 sc) 3 times, FPdc around next 2 sc on row 1, sc in next sc, FPdc around next 2 sc on row 1, sc in last 2 sc.
Row 5: Ch 1, turn; sc in first 2 sc, (work front cable over next 5 sts, sc in next 3 sc) 3 times, work front cable over next 5 sts, sc in last 2 sc.
Row 7: Ch 1, turn; sc in first 2 sc, FPdc around first 2 FPtr, sc in next sc, FPdc around next 2 FPtr, * sc in next 3 sc, FPdc around next 2 FPtr, sc in next sc FPdc around next 2 FPtr; rep from * twice, sc in last 2 sc.
Rows 9 and 11: Ch 1, turn; sc in first 2 sc, FPdc around first 2 FPdc, sc in next 2 sc, * FPdc around next 2 FPdc, sc in next sc, FPdc around next 2 FPdc **, sc in next 3 sc; rep from * 3 times, ending last rep at **, sc in next 2 sc, FPdc around last 2 FPdc, sc in last 2 sc.
Row 13: Ch 1, turn; sc in first 2 sc, FPdc around first 2 FPdc, sc in next 2 sc, (work back cable over next 5 sts, sc in next 3 sc) 3 times, work back cable over next 5 sts, sc in next 2 sc, FPdc around last 2 FPdc, sc in last 2 sc.
Row 15: Ch 1, turn; sc in first 2 sc, FPdc around first 2 FPdc, sc in next 2 sc, * FPdc around next 2 FPtr, sc in next sc, FPdc around next 2 FPtr **, sc in next 3 sc; rep from * 3 times, ending last rep at **, sc in next 2 sc, FPdc around last 2 FPdc, sc in last 2 sc.
Rows 17 and 19: Ch 1, turn; sc in first 2 sc, FPdc around first 2 FPdc, sc in next sc, * FPdc around next 2 FPdc, sc in next 3 sc, FPdc around next 2 FPdc, sc in next sc; rep from * 3 times, FPdc around last 2 FPdc, sc in last 2 sc.
Rows 21–263: Rep rows 5–20, 16 times, then rep rows 5–7 once; fasten off after last row.

Rope Strip (Make 3.)
Ch 33.
Row 1 (rs): Sc in 2nd ch from hook and in ea ch across: 32 sc.
Note: Mark last row as rs.
Row 2 and all Even-Numbered Rows (ws): Ch 1, turn; sc in ea st across.
Row 3: Ch 1, turn; sc in first 2 sc, (FPdc around next 2 sc on row 1, sc in next sc) twice, sc in next sc, FPdc around next sc on row 1, sc in next 2 sc, (FPdc around next 2 sc on row 1, sc in next sc) 3 times, sc in next sc, FPdc around next sc on row 1, sc in next 2 sc, (FPdc around next 2 sc on row 1, sc in next sc) twice, sc in last sc.
Row 5: Ch 1, turn; sc in first 2 sc, work front cable over next 5 sts, sc in next 2 sc, FPdc around next st, sc in next 2 sc, work back cable

(continued)

Project was stitched with Imagine: Fisherman #99.

over next 5 sts, sc in next st, FPdc around next 2 FPdc, sc in next 2 sc, FPdc around next st, sc in next 2 sc, work front cable over next 5 sts, sc in last 2 sc.

Row 7: Ch 1, turn; sc in first 2 sc, * (FPdc around first 2 FPtr, sc in next sc) twice, sc in next sc, FPdc around next FPdc, sc in next 2 sc **, (FPdc around next 2 FPtr, sc in next sc) twice, FPdc around next 2 FPdc, sc in next 2 sc, FPdc around next FPdc, sc in next 2 sc; rep from * to ** once.

Row 9: Ch 1, turn; sc in first 2 sc, work front cable over next 5 sts, sc in next 2 sc, FPdc around next FPdc, sc in next 2 sc, FPdc around

next 2 FPdc, sc in next sc, work front cable over next 5 sts, sc in next 2 sc, FPdc around next FPdc, sc in next 2 sc, work front cable over next 5 sts, sc in last 2 sc.

Row 11: Ch 1, turn; sc in first 2 sc, (FPdc around first 2 FPtr, sc in next sc) twice, sc in next sc, FPdc around next FPdc, sc in next 2 sc, FPdc around next 2 FPdc, (sc in next sc, FPdc around next 2 FPtr) twice, sc in next 2 sc, FPdc around next FPdc, sc in next 2 sc, (FPdc around next 2 FPtr, sc in next sc) twice, sc in last sc.

Rows 13–263: Rep rows 5–12, 31 times, then rep rows 5–7 once; fasten off after last row.

Assembly

Beg and ending with Rope Strips, alternate Rope Strips and Cable Strips. Join 2 strips as folls: With ws tog and working through both thicknesses, join yarn in top corner with sl st, ch 1, sc evenly down long edge to next corner; fasten off.

Border

With rs facing, join yarn in top left corner with sl st, ch 1, sc in same st, sc evenly across to next corner, * 3 sc in corner, sc evenly across to next corner, sl st loosely in ea ch across to next corner; rep from * around, sl st to beg sc; fasten off.

Guernsey

The island of Guernsey has just as much stitching tradition as the Aran Isles. This afghan combines single and triple crochet stitches to make horizontal panels of bobbles.

Materials

Chunky-weight brushed acrylic yarn, approximately: 67½ oz. (3,105 yd.) blue
Sizes H and J crochet hooks or sizes to obtain gauge

Finished Size

Approximately 50" x 64"

Gauge

In pat with larger hook, 12 sts and 12 rows = 4"

With larger hook, ch 150.
Row 1 (rs): Sc in 2nd ch from hook and in ea ch across: 149 sc.
Row 2: Sc in first 2 sc, (tr in next sc, sc in next sc) across to last sc, sc in last sc.

Row 3: Ch 1, turn; sc in first sc and in ea st across.
Row 4: Ch 1, turn; sc in first sc, (tr in next sc, sc in next sc) across.
Row 5: Rep row 3.
Rows 6–27: Rep rows 2–5, 5 times, then rep rows 2 and 3 once.
Row 28 (ws): Ch 2 [counts as first hdc throughout], turn; sk first sc, working in ft lps only, hdc in next st and in ea st across: 149 hdc.
Row 29: Ch 1, turn; working in both lps, sc in first hdc and in ea hdc across: 149 sc.
Row 30: Ch 1, turn; sc in first 2 sc, (tr in next 2 sc, sc in next 2 sc) across to last 3 sc, tr in next 2 sc, sc in last sc.
Row 31: Ch 1, turn; sc in first sc and in ea st across.
Row 32: Ch 1, turn; sc in first 4 sc, (tr in next 2 sc, sc in next 2 sc) across to last sc, sc in last sc.

Row 33: Rep row 31.
Rows 34–53: Rep rows 30–33, 5 times.
Rows 54 and 55: Rep rows 28 and 29.
Rows 56–189: Rep rows 2–55 twice, then rep rows 2–27 once; do not fasten off after last row.

Border

Rnd 1 (rs): With smaller hook, 2 sc in same st, sc evenly across to next corner, * 3 sc in corner, sc evenly across to next corner; rep from * around; join with sl st to beg sc.
Rnd 2: Ch 2, working in bk lps only, 2 hdc in same st, hdc in ea st across to next corner, * 3 hdc in corner, hdc in ea st across to next corner; rep from * around; join with sl st to top of beg ch-2; fasten off.

Project was stitched with Jiffy: Heather Blue #111.

Buttons and Bows

Simple crocheted circles and tiny bows make up this whimsical baby afghan. If you're short on time, just crochet some buttons and stitch them securely on a purchased blanket.

Materials
Sportweight acrylic yarn, approximately:
13½ oz. (1,530 yd.) pastel green-and-yellow variegated, MC
5½ oz. (590 yd.) light green, A
3½ oz. (395 yd.) light yellow, B
Sizes G and F crochet hooks or sizes to obtain gauge
Yarn needle

Finished Size
Approximately 37" x 38"

Gauge
With larger hook, 9 sc and 9 rows = 2"

Pattern Stitch
Puff: (Yo, insert hook in st indicated, yo and pull up lp) 3 times, yo and draw through all 7 lps on hook.

Note: To change colors, work last yo of prev st with new color, dropping prev color to ws of work.

With larger hook and MC, ch 164.
Row 1 (rs): Sc in 2nd ch from hook and in ea ch across: 163 sc.
Rows 2–8: Ch 1, turn; sc in first sc and in ea sc across.
Row 9: Ch 1, turn; sc in first sc and in ea sc across, change to A in last st.

Row 10: Ch 1, turn; sc in first sc, ch 1, sk next sc, sc in next sc, * sk next sc, (2 dc, ch 2, sc) in next sc, puff in next sc, (sc, ch 2, 2 dc) in next sc, sk next sc, sc in next sc, ch 1, sk next sc, sc in next sc; rep from * across, changing to MC in last sc.
Row 11: Ch 3 [counts as first dc throughout], turn; sk first sc, dc in next ch-1 sp, * ch 1, sk next dc, sc in next dc, ch 3, sc in next dc, ch 1, sk next sc, dc in next ch-1 sp; rep from * across to last st, dc in last st.
Row 12: Ch 1, turn; sc in first 2 dc, * sc in next ch-1 sp, sc in next sc, 3 sc in next ch-3 sp, sc in next sc, sc in next ch-1 sp, sc in next dc; rep from * across to last dc, sc in last dc: 163 sc.
Rows 13 and 14: Rep row 2 twice.
Row 15: Ch 1, turn; sc in first sc and in ea sc across, change to B in last st.
Row 16: With B, rep row 10.
Rows 17 and 18: Rep rows 11 and 12 once.
Rows 19 and 20: Rep row 2 twice.
Rows 21–24: Rep rows 9–12 once.
Rows 25–171: Rep rows 2–24, 6 times, then rep row 2, 9 times; fasten off after last row.

Border
Rnd 1 (rs): With rs facing and smaller hook, join MC in top right corner with sl st, sc in same st and in ea st across to corner, 3 sc in corner, * sc evenly across to next corner, 3 sc in next corner; rep from * around; join with sl st to beg sc; fasten off.
Rnd 2 (ws): With ws facing, join A in corner sc with sl st, ch 1, sc in same sc, ch 1, * sk next sc, (2 dc, ch 2, sc) in next sc, puff in next sc, (sc, ch 2, 2 dc) in next sc, sk next sc, sc in next sc, change to B, sc in next sc; sk next sc, (2 dc, ch 2, sc) in next sc, puff in next sc, (sc, ch 2, 2 dc) in next sc, sk next sc, sc in next sc, change to A; rep from * around; join with sl st to beg sc; fasten off.

Button (Make 68 ea with A and B.)
With larger hook, ch 3, sl st to form ring.
Rnd 1 (rs): Ch 1, 7 sc in ring; join with sl st to beg sc: 7 sc.
Note: Mark last rnd as rs.
Rnd 2: Ch 2, 2 hdc in first sc and in ea sc around; join with sl st to beg hdc; fasten off: 14 hdc.

Assembly
With rs facing and referring to photo, arrange 17 Buttons in ea sc section, alternating colors. Using 2 strands of contrasting color, sew ea button to afghan with large cross-stitch.

Project was stitched with Jamie Baby: Sherbet Print #239, Pastel Green #269, and Pastel Yellow #257.

Southwestern Diamonds

The vibrant colors and strong design of this afghan remind me of the gorgeous blankets woven by Native Americans.

Materials

Worsted-weight wool-blend
  yarn, approximately:
15 oz. (985 yd.) black, MC
12 oz. (790 yd.) teal green, A
20 oz. (1,300 yd.) fuchsia-and-
  brown variegated, B
Size K crochet hook or size to
  obtain gauge

Finished Size

Approximately 48" x 70"

Gauge

13 sc and 15 rows = 4"

Note: To change colors, work last yo of prev st with new color, dropping prev color to ws of work. Do not carry yarn across row.

With MC, ch 148.
Row 1 (rs): Sc in 2nd ch from hook and in next 5 sc, (change to B, sc in next 27 sc, change to MC, sc in next 9 sc) 3 times, change to B, sc in next 27 sc, change to MC, sc in last 6 sc: 147 sc.
Row 2 (ws): Ch 1 turn; sc in first 5 sc, (change to B, sc in next 29 sc, change to MC, sc in next 7 sc) 3 times, change to B, sc in next 29 sc, change to MC, sc in last 6 sc.
Rows 3–46: Cont foll *Chart* as est, reading odd (rs) rows from right to left and even (ws) rows from left to right.
Rows 47–250: Rep rows 1–46, 4 times, then rep rows 1–20 once; fasten off after last row.

Border

Rnd 1 (rs): With rs facing, join MC in top right corner with sl st, ch 1, sc in same st and in ea st across to corner, * 3 sc in corner, sc evenly across to next corner; rep from * around; join with sl st to beg sc.
Rnd 2: Ch 1, sc in same st and in ea st across to corner, * 3 sc in corner, sc in ea st across to next corner; rep from * around; join with sl st to beg sc; fasten off.
Rnd 3: With rs facing, join A in top right corner with sl st, ch 1, sc in same st and in ea st across to corner, * 3 sc in corner, sc evenly across to next corner; rep from * around; join with sl st to beg sc.
Rnd 4: Rep rnd 2.
Rnd 5: Rep rnd 1.
Rnds 6–8: Ch 1, sc in same st and in ea st across to corner, * 3 sc in corner, sc in ea st across to next corner; rep from * around; join with sl st to beg sc; fasten off after last rnd.

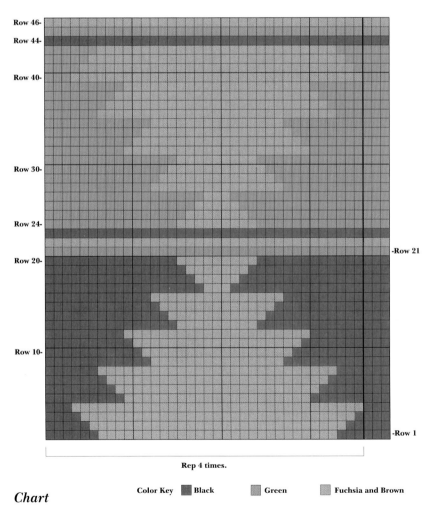

Chart

Color Key ■ Black ■ Green ■ Fuchsia and Brown

Rep 4 times.

Project was stitched with Wool-Ease: Black #153, Hunter Green #132, and Country Print #231.

Afghan-Stitch Stripes

Since each row of afghan stitch is worked in two steps, you can create subtle color changes by working the first step in one color and the second step in another.

Materials
Worsted-weight alpaca-wool-acrylic blend yarn, approximately:
10½ oz. (645 yd.) dark brown, MC
17½ oz. (1,070 yd.) light brown, A
8¾ oz. (535 yd.) ecru, B
Size K afghan hook or size to obtain gauge
Size J crochet hook

Finished Size
Approximately 49" x 56"

Gauge
15 sts and 11 rows = 4"

Note: See page 142 for afghan st directions. To change colors, work last yo of prev st with new color, dropping prev color to ws of work.

With MC and afghan hook, ch 181.
Rows 1–3: With MC, work 3 rows of afghan st.
Row 4: Work Step 1 with MC, change to A, work Step 2 with A.
Row 5: Work Step 1 with A, change to MC, work Step 2 with MC.
Row 6: Rep row 4.
Rows 7–9: With A, work 3 rows of afghan st.
Row 10: Work Step 1 with A, change to B, work Step 2 with B.
Row 11: Work Step 1 with B, change to A, work Step 2 with A.

Row 12: Rep row 10.
Rows 13–15: With B, work 3 rows of afghan st.
Row 16: Rep row 11.
Row 17: Rep row 10.
Row 18: Rep row 11.
Rows 19–21: Rep rows 7–9 once.
Row 22: Rep row 5.
Row 23: Rep row 4.
Row 24: Rep row 5.
Rows 25–147: Rep rows 1–24, 5 times, then rep rows 1–3 once; sl st in ea vertical bar across; fasten off.

Border
Rnd 1 (rs): With rs facing and crochet hook, join A in top right corner with sl st, ch 1, 3 sc in same st, sc evenly across to next corner, * 3 sc in corner, sc evenly across to next corner; rep from * around; join with sl st to beg sc.
Rnd 2: Ch 1, working from left to right, sc in same st and in ea sc around [reverse sc]; join with sl st to beg sc; fasten off.

Project was stitched with Al•Pa•Ka: Mink Brown #127, Camel #124, and Natural #98.

Pink Pineapples

Take a traditional doily motif and turn it into a lacy throw. The tiny picots edging this afghan are a delicate finish.

Materials
Sportweight acrylic yarn, approximately:
28 oz. (3,140 yd.) pink
Size G crochet hook or size to obtain gauge

Finished Size
Approximately 54" x 66"

Gauge
In pat, 1 pat rep and 7 rows = 3½"

Ch 229.

Row 1 (rs): 2 dc in 4th ch from hook, * ch 7, sk next 5 chs, sc in next ch, ch 3, sk next 2 chs, sc in next ch, ch 7, sk next 5 chs **, (2 dc, ch 1, 2 dc) in next ch [shell made]; rep from * across, ending last rep at **, 3 dc in last ch: 15 ch-3 sps.

Row 2: Ch 3 [counts as first dc throughout], turn; 2 dc in first dc, * ch 3, sc in next ch-7 sp, ch 5, sk next ch-3 sp, sc in next ch-7 sp, ch 3 **, shell in top of next shell [ch-1 sp]; rep from * across, ending last rep at **, 3 dc in top of tch: 15 ch-5 sps.

Row 3: Ch 3, turn; 2 dc in first dc, * sk next ch-3 sp, 11 tr in next ch-5 sp **, shell in top of next shell; rep from * across, ending last rep at **, 3 dc in top of tch.

Row 4: Ch 3, turn; 2 dc in first dc, * ch 2, sc in next tr, (ch 3, sk next tr, sc in next tr) 5 times, ch 2 **, shell in top of next shell; rep from * across, ending last rep at **, 3 dc in top of tch.

Row 5: Ch 3, turn; 2 dc in first dc, * (ch 3, sc in next ch-3 sp) 5 times, ch 3 **, shell in top of next shell; rep from * across, ending last rep at **, 3 dc in top of tch.

Row 6: Ch 3 turn; 2 dc in first dc, * ch 4, sk next ch-3 sp, sc in next ch-3 sp, (ch 3, sc in next ch-3 sp) 3 times, ch 4 **, shell in top of next shell; rep from * across, ending last rep at **, 3 dc in top of tch.

Row 7: Ch 3, turn; 2 dc in first dc, * ch 5, sc in next ch-3 sp, (ch 3, sc in next ch-3 sp) twice, ch 5 **, shell in top of next shell; rep from * across, ending last rep at **, 3 dc in top of tch.

Row 8: Ch 3, turn; 2 dc in first dc, * ch 7, sc in next ch-3 sp, ch 3, sc in next ch-3 sp, ch 7 **, shell in top of next shell; rep from * across, ending last rep at **, 3 dc in top of tch.

Row 9: Ch 3, turn; 2 dc in first dc, * ch 1, shell in next ch-7 sp, ch 1, sk next ch-3 sp, shell in next ch-7 sp, ch 1 **, shell in top of

next shell; rep from * across, ending last rep at **, 3 dc in top of tch: 44 shells.

Rows 10–18: Ch 3, turn; 2 dc in first dc, ch 1, (shell in top of next shell, ch 1) across, 3 dc in top of tch.

Row 19: Ch 3, turn; 2 dc in first dc, * ch 7, sk next 5 dc, sc in next dc, ch 3, sk next dc, sc in next dc, ch 7 **, shell in top of next shell; rep from * across, ending last rep at **, 3 dc in last ch: 15 ch-3 sps.

Rows 20–128: Rep rows 2–18, 6 times, then rep rows 2–8 once.

Row 129: Ch 1, turn; sc in first dc, hdc in next dc, * ch 3, sk next dc, 2 sc in next ch-7 sp, ch 3, sk next ch-3 sp, 2 sc in next ch-7 sp, ch 3, sk next dc **, sc in next dc, ch 1, sc in next dc; rep from * across, ending last rep at **, hdc in next dc, sc in top of tch.

Border

Rnd 1 (ws): Ch 1, turn; 3 sc in first sc, sc in ea sc evenly across to next corner, * 3 sc in corner, sc evenly across to next corner; rep from * around; join with sl st to beg sc.

Rnd 2 (rs): Ch 3, turn; dc in next sc and in ea sc across to next corner, * 3 dc in corner, dc in ea sc across to next corner; rep from * around; join with sl st to top of tch.

Rnd 3: Ch 1, turn; sc in first 2 dc, * ch 2, sl st in second ch from hook, ch 1, sk next dc, sc in next 2 dc; rep from * around; join with sl st to beg sc; fasten off.

Country Plaid

Create a simple plaid with deeply colored stripes for down-home appeal. The small motifs appliquéd between the stripes are optional.

Materials
Worsted-weight wool-blend yarn, approximately:
39 oz. (2,565 yd.) cream, MC
12 oz. (790 yd.) navy, A
3 oz. (200 yd.) red, B
Sizes H and N crochet hooks or sizes to obtain gauge
Yarn needle

Finished Size
Approximately 48" x 51", without fringe

Gauge
With larger hook and holding 2 strands tog, 10 sts and 11 rows = 4"
Star = 3"

Note: Afghan is worked holding 2 strands of yarn tog throughout. To change colors, work last yo of prev st with new color, dropping prev color to ws of work. Work in foll color sequence: * 2 rows MC, 2 rows A, 2 rows MC, 2 rows B, 2 rows MC, 2 rows A **, 16 rows MC; rep from * 4 times more, then rep from * to ** once more, 2 rows MC.

With larger hook and 2 strands of MC, ch 121.
Row 1 (rs): Sc in 2nd ch from hook and in next 2 chs, * (ch 1, sk next ch, sc in next 3 chs) twice, ch 1, sk next ch, sc in next 12 chs; rep from * across to last 12 chs, (ch 1, sk next ch, sc in next 3 chs) 3 times: 18 ch-1 sps.
Row 2: Ch 1, turn; sc in first 3 sc, * ch 1, sk next ch-1 sp, sc in next 3 sc) twice, ch 1, sk next ch-1 sp, sc in next 12 sc; rep from * across to last 9 sc, (ch 1, sk next ch-1 sp, sc in next 3 sc) 3 times: 18 ch-1 sps.
Rows 3–140: Rep row 2, 138 times, foll color sequence; fasten off after last row.

Stripes
Stripe 1: With rs facing and larger hook, join 2 strands of A in bottom right ch-1 sp with sl st; working vertically, sl st in ea ch-1 sp to top edge; fasten off, leaving 3" tail.
Stripe 2: With rs facing and larger hook, join 2 strands of B in next ch-1 sp along bottom edge with sl st; working vertically, sl st in ea ch-1 sp to top edge; fasten off, leaving 3" tail.
Stripes 3 and 4: With rs facing and larger hook, join 2 strands of A in next ch-1 sp along bottom edge with sl st; working vertically, sl st in ea ch-1 sp to top edge; fasten off, leaving 3" tail.
Stripes 5–18: Rep stripes 2–4, 4 times, then rep stripes 2 and 3 once.

Star (Make 13.)
With smaller hook and 1 strand A, ch 3, join with sl st to form ring.
Rnd 1 (rs): Ch 1, 6 sc in ring; join with sl st to beg sc: 6 sc.

Note: Mark last rnd as rs.
Rnd 2: Ch 1, 2 sc in ea sc around; join with sl st to beg sc: 12 sc.
Rnd 3: Ch 1, 2 sc in ea sc around; join with sl st to beg sc: 24 sc.
Rnd 4: Ch 1, sc in first sc, * ch 1, dc in next sc, ch 1, tr in next sc, ch 1, dc in next sc, ch 1 **, sc in next 2 sc; rep from * around, ending last rep at **, sc in next sc; join with sl st to beg sc; fasten off.

Referring to page 142 of General Directions and using 1 strand of B, blanket-stitch around ea star.

Assembly
Referring to photo, sew stars to afghan as desired.

Fringe
Referring to page 143 of General Directions, for ea top and bottom edge tassel, cut 2 (6") lengths of yarn. Working across top and bottom edges and matching colors, knot 1 tassel in end of ea stripe, securing 3" tail within ea tassel.

For ea side edge tassel, cut 3 (6") lengths of yarn. Working along side edges and matching colors, knot 1 tassel in end of ea stripe.

Project was stitched with Wool-Ease: Ivory Sprinkles #97, Navy Sprinkles #110, and Red Sprinkles #112.

Lattice Clusters

Brighten a moody music room or a dark den with a splashy colored throw. A medley of clusters and diagonal post stitches compose this afghan.

Materials
Worsted-weight mohair-blend yarn, approximately:
30 oz. (2,665 yd.) dark rose
Size J crochet hook or size needed for gauge

Finished Size
Approximately 40" x 52", without fringe

Gauge
In pat, 13 sts and 14½ rows = 4"

Pattern Stitches
Cl: (Yo, insert hook in st indicated, yo and pull up lp, yo and draw through 2 lps) 4 times, yo and draw through all 5 lps on hook.
Front Post tr (FPtr): Yo twice, insert hook from front to back around post of next st, yo and pull up lp, (yo and pull through 2 lps) 3 times.

Ch 129.
Row 1 (rs): Sc in 2nd ch from hook and in ea ch across: 128 sc.
Rows 2–4: Ch 1, turn; sc in first sc and in ea sc across.
Row 5: Ch 1, turn; sc in first 3 sc, working in front of last 3 sts, FPtr around 2nd sc on row 1, sk next 5 sc on row 1, FPtr around next sc on row 1, sk next 2 sc on row 5, * sc in next 2 sc, cl in next sc, sc in next 2 sc, FPtr around next sc after last FPtr on row 1, sk next 5 sc on row 1, FPtr around next sc on row 1, sk next 2 sc on row 5; rep from * across to last 4 sc, sc in last 4 sc: 17 cls.
Rows 6–8: Rep rows 2–4.
Row 9: Ch 1, turn; sc in first sc, FPtr around 4th sc on row 6, sk next sc on row 9, * sc in next 2 sc, cl in next sc, sc in next 2 sc, FPtr around next sc after last FPtr on row 6 **, sk 5 sc on row 6, FPtr around next sc on row 6, sk next 2 sc on row 9; rep from * across to last 2 sc, ending last rep at **, sk next sc on row 9, sc in last sc: 18 cls.
Rows 10–12: Rep rows 2–4.
Row 13: Ch 1, turn; sc in first 3 sc, working in front of last 3 sts, FPtr around 2nd sc on row 10, sk next 5 sc on row 10, FPtr around next sc on row 10, sk next 2 sc on row 5, * sc in next 2 sc, cl in next sc, sc in next 2 sc, FPtr around next sc after last FPtr on row 10, sk next 5 sc on row 10, FPtr around next sc on row 10, sk next 2 sc on row 5; rep from * across to last 4 sc, sc in last 4 sc.
Rows 14–184: Rep rows 6–13, 21 times, then rep rows 6–8 once.
Row 185: Ch 1, turn; sc in first sc, FPtr around 4th sc on row 182, sk next sc on row 185, * sc in next 5 sc, FPtr around next sc after last FPtr on row 182 **, sk 5 sc on row 182, FPtr around next sc on row 182, sk next 2 sc on row 185; rep from * across to last 2 sc, ending last rep at **, sk next sc on row 185, sc in last sc; fasten off.

Border
Rnd 1 (rs): With rs facing, join yarn in top right corner with sl st, ch 1, sc in same st and in ea st across to next corner, * 3 sc in corner, sc evenly across to next corner; rep from * around; join with sl st to beg sc.
Rnd 2: Ch 1, sc in same st and in ea st across to corner, * 3 sc in corner, sc in ea st across to next corner; rep from * around; join with sl st to beg sc; fasten off.

Fringe
For ea tassel, referring to page 143 of General Directions, cut 5 (16") lengths of yarn. Working across short ends, knot 1 tassel in every 4th st.

Project was stitched with Imagine: Rose #139.

Ripples with Ridges

This variation on a classic ripple softens the peaks and adds post stitches to them. Between the peaks, the darkest color weaves in and out.

Materials

Worsted-weight wool-blend yarn, approximately:
15 oz. (985 yd.) dark rose, MC
15 oz. (985 yd.) medium rose, A
15 oz. (985 yd.) light rose, B
6 oz. (395 yd.) burgundy, C
Size H crochet hook or size to obtain gauge
Yarn needle

Finished Size

Approximately 55" x 59", without fringe

Gauge

In pat, 24 sts and 10 rows = 6"

Pattern Stitches

Front Post dc (FPdc): Yo, insert hook from front to back around post of st indicated, yo and pull up lp, (yo and pull through 2 lps) twice; sk st behind FPdc.

Back Post dc (BPdc): Yo, insert hook from back to front around post of st indicated, yo and pull up lp, (yo and pull through 2 lps) twice; sk st behind BPdc.

Inc: 3 dc in st indicated.

Dec: Yo, insert hook in st indicated, yo and pull up lp, yo and draw through 2 lps, sk next st, yo, insert hook in next st, yo and pull up lp, yo and draw through 2 lps, yo and draw through all 3 lps on hook.

Note: To change colors, work last yo of prev st with new color, dropping prev color to ws of work. Do not carry yarn across row.

With MC, ch 221.
Row 1 (ws): Dc in 4th ch from hook, * dc in next ch, inc, dc in next 2 chs, ch 1, sk next ch, dc in next 2 chs, dec in next ch, dc in next 3 chs, dec in next ch, dc in next 2 chs, ch 1, sk next ch, dc in next 2 chs, inc in next ch, dc in next 2 chs; rep from * across to last ch, dc in last ch, change to A: 219 sts.
Row 2 (rs): With A, ch 3, turn; sk first dc, * FPdc around next dc,

dc in next dc, inc in next dc, dc in next 2 dc, ch 1, sk next dc, dc in next dc, dc in next ch-1 sp, dec in next dc, dc in next dc, FPdc around next dc, dc in next dc, dec in next dc, dc in next ch-1 sp, dc in next dc, ch 1, sk next dc, dc in next 2 dc, inc in next dc, dc in next dc; rep from * across to last dc, FPdc around next dc, dc in top of beg ch-3, change to B.
Row 3: With B, ch 3, turn; sk first dc, * BPdc around first FPdc, dc in next dc, inc in next dc, dc in next 2 dc, ch 1, sk next dc, dc in next dc, dc in next ch-1 sp, dec

(continued)

Project was stitched with Wool-Ease: Dark Rose Heather #139, Rose Heather #140, Blush Heather #104, and Burgundy Sprinkles #142.

in next dc, dc in next dc, BPdc around next FPdc, dc in next dc, dec in next dc, dc in next ch-1 sp, dc in next dc, ch 1, sk next dc, dc in next 2 dc, inc in next dc, dc in next dc; rep from * across to last FPdc, BPdc around FPdc, dc in top of beg ch-3, change to MC.

Row 4: With MC, ch 3, turn; sk first dc, * FPdc around first BPdc, dc in next dc, inc in next dc, dc in next 2 dc, ch 1, sk next dc, dc in next dc, dc in next ch-1 sp, dec in next dc, dc in next dc, FPdc around next BPdc, dc in next dc, dec in next dc, dc in next ch-1 sp, dc in next dc, ch 1, sk next dc, dc in next 2 dc, inc in next dc, dc in next dc; rep from * across to last BPdc, FPdc around BPdc, dc in top of beg ch-3, change to A.

Row 5: With A, rep row 3, changing to B in last st.

Row 6: With B, rep row 4, changing to MC in last st.

Row 7: With MC, rep row 3, changing to A in last st.

Row 8: With A, rep row 4, changing to B in last st.

Rows 9–97: Rep rows 3–8, 14 times, then rep rows 3–7 once; fasten off MC and B.

Border

With A, ch 1, turn; with ws facing, sc in ea st and ch-1 sp across to last sc, 2 sc in last st, sc evenly across to next corner, 2 sc in corner, sc in free lp of ea foundation ch across to next corner, 2 sc in corner, sc evenly across to next corner, sc in corner; join with sl st to beg sc; fasten off.

Weaving

With D, and leaving 6" tails, crochet a 66" chain; fasten off. Make 18 chains.

Row 1 (rs): With rs facing, using yarn needle, and working vertically from bottom edge of afghan, weave 1 chain up in first ch-1 sp, * down in next ch-1 sp, up in next ch-1 sp; rep from * across; fasten off.

Rows 2–18: Rep row 1, beg in next ch-1 sp.

Fringe

For ea tassel, referring to page 143 of General Directions, cut 12 (12") lengths of D. Working across short ends, knot 1 tassel at ea end of ea woven chain. Rep with rem chains.

Because the ripples are soft and do not come to exact points, you must count very carefully when stitching this afghan.

Granny's Flowers

Combine elegant flower motifs with oversize granny squares. The scalloped border echoes the flower petals.

Materials

Worsted-weight mohair-blend
   yarn, approximately:
15 oz. (1,335 yd.) white, MC
10 oz. (890 yd.) blue, CC
Size J crochet hook or size to
   obtain gauge

Finished Size

Approximately 42" x 56"

Gauge

Ea Square = 7"

Granny Square (Make 18.)

With CC, ch 4, join with sl st to
form ring.

Rnd 1 (rs): Ch 3 [counts as first dc
throughout], 2 dc in ring, (ch 3,
3 dc in ring) 3 times, ch 3; join
with sl st to top of beg ch-3.
Note: Mark last rnd as rs.

Rnd 2: Sl st in next 2 dc, sl st in
next ch-3 sp, (ch 3, 2 dc, ch 3,
3 dc) in same ch-3 sp, * ch 2,
(3 dc, ch 3, 3 dc) in next ch-3 sp;
rep from * around, ch 2; join with
sl st to top of beg ch.

Rnd 3: Sl st in next 2 dc, sl st in
next ch-3 sp, (ch 3, 2 dc, ch 3,
3 dc) in same ch-3 sp, * ch 2,
3 dc in next ch-2 sp, ch 2 **,
(3 dc, ch 3, 3 dc) in next ch-3 sp;
rep from * around, ending last
rep at **; join with sl st to top of
beg ch.

Rnd 4: Sl st in next 2 dc, sl st in
next ch-3 sp, (ch 3, 2 dc, ch 3,
3 dc) in same ch-3 sp, * (ch 2,
3 dc in next ch-2 sp) twice, ch 2 **,
(3 dc, ch 3, 3 dc) in next ch-3 sp;
rep from * around, ending last
rep at **; join with sl st to top of
beg ch.

Rnd 5: Sl st in next 2 dc, sl st in
next ch-3 sp, (ch 3, 2 dc, ch 3,
3 dc) in same ch-3 sp, * (ch 2,
3 dc in next ch-2 sp) 3 times,
ch 2 **, (3 dc, ch 3, 3 dc) in next
ch-3 sp; rep from * around, ending last rep at **; join with sl st to
top of beg ch.

Rnd 6: Sl st in next 2 dc, sl st in
next ch-3 sp, (ch 3, 2 dc, ch 3,
3 dc) in same ch-3 sp, * (ch 2,
3 dc in next ch-2 sp) 4 times,
ch 2 **, (3 dc, ch 3, 3 dc) in next
ch-3 sp; rep from * around, ending last rep at **; join with sl st to
top of beg ch; fasten off.

Flower Square (Make 17.)

With MC, ch 6, join with sl st to
form ring.

Rnd 1 (rs): Ch 3 [counts as first dc
throughout], 15 dc in ring; join
with sl st to beg ch-3: 16 dc.
Note: Mark last rnd as rs.

Rnd 2: Ch 7 [counts as first tr plus
ch 3], sk first 2 dc, (tr in next dc,
ch 3, sk next dc) 7 times; join with
sl st to 4th ch of beg ch-7: 8
ch-3 sps.

Rnd 3: Ch 1, * (hdc, dc, tr, dc,
hdc) in next ch-3 sp [petal made];
rep from * around; join with sl st
to beg hdc: 8 petals.

Rnd 4: Ch 1, sc in same st, * ch 6,
sc in sp between next 2 hdc; rep
from * around, ch 6; join with sl st
to beg sc: 8 ch-6 sps.

Project was stitched with Imagine: White #100 and Blue Heather #111.

Rnd 5: Ch 1, * (hdc, dc, 5 tr, dc, hdc) in next ch-6 sp [petal made]; rep from * around; join with sl st to beg hdc: 8 petals.

Rnd 6: Ch 1, sl st in first dc, sl st in first tr, ch 9 [counts as first dc plus ch 6], * sk next 3 tr, dc in next tr, ch 6 **, sk next 4 sts, dc in next tr; rep from * around, ending last rep at **; join with sl st to 3rd ch of beg ch-9: 16 ch-6 sps.

Rnd 7: Sl st in first ch-6 sp, ch 3, (3 dc, ch 4, 4 dc) in same ch-6 sp [corner made], * ch 4, sc in next ch-6 sp, (ch 6, sc in next ch-6 sp) twice, ch 4 **, (4 dc, ch 4, 4 dc) in next ch-6 sp [corner made]; rep from * around, ending last rep at **; join with sl st to top of beg ch-3; fasten off.

Assembly

Afghan is 7 squares long and 5 squares wide. Whipstitch squares tog in checkerboard pattern.

Edging

Note: Edging is worked sideways and attached to afghan as you go.

With MC, ch 5, join with sl st to corner of afghan.

Row 1: (Dc, ch 2, dc) in 4th ch from hook, (ch 2, dc) twice in last ch.

Row 2: Ch 5, turn; sk first ch-2 sp, dc in next ch-2 sp, (ch 2, dc) 3 times in same ch-2 sp, ch 1, join to Afghan with sl st so that Edging lies flat [approximately every ch-sp].

Row 3: Ch 1, turn; sk first ch-2 sp, dc in next ch-2 sp, (ch 2, dc) 3 times in same ch-2 sp.

Rep rows 2 and 3 alternately across to corner; * (rep rows 2 and 3) 3 times in corner, joining with sl st in same corner; rep rows 2 and 3 alternately across to next corner; rep from * around, (rep rows 2 and 3) twice in last corner; fasten off.

Sew first and last rows tog.

Note: Beg working in rnds.

Rnd 1: Join MC in corner ch-5 sp with sl st, ch 1, sc in same ch-5 sp, * ch 2, (tr, ch 1) 6 times in next ch-5 sp, tr in same ch-5 sp, ch 2 **, sc in next ch-5 sp; rep from * around, ending last rep at **; join with sl st to first sc.

Rnd 2: Ch 1, sk first ch-2 sp, * (sc in next ch-1 sp, ch 3) 5 times, sc in next ch-1 sp, ch 1, sc in next sc, ch 1; rep from * around; join with sl st to beg ch; fasten off.

The attractive edging on this afghan is worked in an unusual manner. Instead of working entirely in rounds, you must first work in rows. This is similar to making lace and attaching it as it is made. Once you've attached the lace, finish it with two rounds to create the scallops.

Milky Way Star

Want to feel like a star crocheter? Combine single crochet and easy loop stitches for stellar results.

Materials
Chunky-weight acrylic yarn, approximately:
36 oz. (1,110 yd.) blue, MC
18 oz. (555 yd.) cream, CC
Size K crochet hook or size to obtain gauge

Finished Size
Approximately 45" x 57"

Gauge
10 sc and 10 rows = 4"

Note: See page 141 for lp st directions. To change colors, work yo of last st in prev color with new color. Do not carry yarn not in use across row.

Center Square (Make 1.)
With CC, ch 31.
Row 1 (rs): Sc in 2nd ch from hook and in ea ch across: 30 sc.
Note: Mark last row as rs.
Row 2 (ws): Ch 1, turn; lp st in first sc and in ea sc across: 30 lp sts.
Row 3: Ch 1, turn; sc in first st and in ea st across.
Rows 4–31: Rep rows 2 and 3 alternately; fasten off after last row.

North Point (Make 1.)
With CC, ch 31.
Row 1 (rs): Sc in 2nd ch and in ea ch across: 30 sc.
Note: Mark last row as rs.
Row 2 (ws): Ch 1, turn; lp st in first 29 sts, change to MC, sc in last st.

Row 3: Ch 1, turn; sc in first 2 sts, change to CC, sc in last 28 sts.
Row 4: Ch 1, turn; lp st in first 27 sts, change to MC, sc in last 3 sts.
Row 5: Ch 1, turn; sc in first 4 sts, change to CC, sc in last 26 sts.
Rows 6–31: Cont in pat, moving color change by 1 st ea row; fasten off after last row.

South Point (Make 1.)
With MC, ch 31.
Row 1 (rs): Sc in 2nd ch from hook and in ea ch across: 30 sc.
Note: Mark last row as rs.
Row 2 (ws): Ch 1, turn; sc in first 29 sts, change to CC, lp st in last st: 1 lp st.
Row 3: Ch 1, turn; sc in first 2 sts, change to MC, sc in next 28 sts.
Row 4: Ch 1, turn; sc in next 27 sts, change to CC, lp st in last 3 sts.
Row 5: Ch 1, turn; sc in next 4 sts, change to MC, sc in next 26 sts.
Rows 6–31: Cont in pat, moving color change by 1 st ea row; fasten off after last row.

East Point (Make 1.)
With MC, ch 31.
Row 1 (rs): Sc in 2nd ch from hook and in ea ch across, change to CC: 30 sc.
Note: Mark last row as rs.
Row 2 (ws): With CC, ch 1, turn; lp st in first st, change to MC, sc next st and in ea st across: 1 lp st.
Row 3: Ch 1, turn; sc in first 28 sc, change to CC, sc in last 2 sts.
Row 4: Ch 1, turn; lp st in first

3 sts, change to MC, sc in next 27 sts.
Row 5: Ch 1, turn; sc in next 26 sts, change to CC, sc in next 24 sts.
Rows 6–31: Cont in pat, moving color change by 1 st ea row; fasten off after last row.

West Point (Make 1.)
With CC, ch 31.
Row 1 (rs): Sc in 2nd ch from hook and in ea ch across, change to MC: 30 sc.
Note: Mark last row as rs.
Row 2 (ws): With MC, ch 1, turn; sc in first st, change to CC, lp st in next st and in ea st across: 29 lp sts.
Row 3: Ch 1, turn; sc in first 28 sts, change to MC, sc in last 2 sts.
Row 4: Ch 1, turn; sc in next 3 sts, change to CC, lp st in next 27 sts.
Row 5: Ch 1, turn; sc in first 26 sts, change to MC, sc in last 4 sts.
Rows 6–31: Cont in pat, moving color change by 1 st ea row; fasten off after last row.

Solid Square (Make 4.)
With MC, ch 31.
Row 1 (rs): Sc in 2nd ch from hook and in ea ch across: 30 sc.
Note: Mark last row as rs.
Rows 2–31: Ch 1, turn; sc in first sc and in ea sc across: 30 sc; fasten off after last row.

(continued)

Project was stitched with Homespun: Colonial #302 and Deco #309.

Half Square (Make 6.)

With MC, ch 31.

Row 1 (rs): Sc in 2nd ch from hook and in ea ch across: 30 sc.

Note: Mark last row as rs.

Rows 2–15: Ch 1, turn; sc in first sc and in ea sc across: 30 sc; fasten off after last row.

Assembly

Referring to *Placement Diagram,* whipstitch blocks tog.

Border

Rnd 1 (rs): With rs facing, join MC to top right corner with sl st, ch 1, sc in same st, sc evenly across to next corner, * 3 sc in corner, sc evenly across to next corner; rep from * around; join with sl st to beg sc; fasten off.

Rnd 2: With rs facing, join CC to top right corner with sl st, ch 1, sc in same st and in ea st across to corner, * 3 sc in corner, sc in ea st across to next corner; rep from * around; join with sl st to beg sc.

For the best results, measure each loop stitch carefully. If you maintain consistent stitches, your afghan will have an even texture.

Rnd 3: Ch 1, sc in same st and in ea st across to corner, * 3 sc in corner, sc in ea st across to next corner; rep from * around; join with sl st to beg sc; fasten off.

Rnd 4: With rs facing, join MC to top right corner with sl st, ch 1, sc in same st and in ea st across to corner, * 3 sc in corner, sc in ea st across to next corner; rep from * around; join with sl st to beg sc.

Rnds 5–7: Ch 1, sc in same st and in ea st across to corner, * 3 sc in corner, sc in ea st across to next corner; rep from * around; join with sl st to beg sc. Fasten off after last rnd.

Rnds 8–13: Rep rnds 2–7 once.

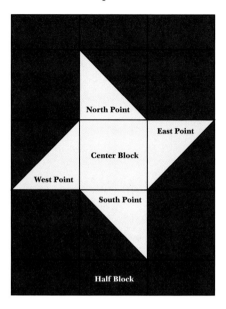

Placement Diagram

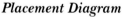

Sweetheart Shells

Make a precious baby afghan with stripes of shell stitches and heart-shaped appliqués.

Materials

Sportweight acrylic yarn, approximately:
8¾ oz. (980 yd.) white, MC
5¼ oz. (590 yd.) pink, CC
Sizes F and G crochet hooks or sizes to obtain gauge
Yarn needle

Finished Size

Approximately 34" x 34"

Gauge

In pat with larger hook, 19 sts and 12 rows = 4"

Note: To change colors, work last yo of prev st with new color, dropping prev color to ws of work.

With larger hook and MC, ch 154.
Row 1 (ws): Sc in 2nd ch from hook, * sk next ch, 3 dc in next ch, sk next ch, sc in next ch; rep from * across.
Row 2 (rs): Ch 4 [counts as first dc plus ch 1 throughout], turn; sk first sc, sk next dc, sc in next dc, ch 1, sk next dc, dc in next sc, * ch 1, sk next dc, sc in next dc, ch 1, sk next dc, dc in next sc; rep from * across, changing to CC in last dc.
Row 3: With CC, ch 1, turn; sc in first dc, * sk next ch-1 sp, 3 dc in next sc, sk next ch-1 sp, sc in next dc; rep from * across.
Row 4: Ch 4, turn; sk first sc, sk next dc, sc in next dc, ch 1, sk next dc, dc in next sc, * ch 1, sk next dc, sc in next dc, ch 1, sk next dc, dc in next sc; rep from * across, changing to MC in last dc.
Row 5: With MC, ch 1, turn; sc in first dc, * sk next ch-1 sp, 3 dc in next sc, sk next ch-1 sp, sc in next dc; rep from * across.

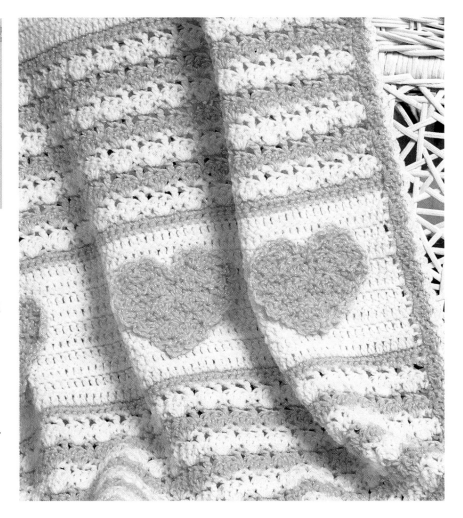

Rows 6–14: Rep rows 2–5 twice, then rep row 2 once.
Note: Change to smaller hook.
Row 15: With smaller hook and CC, ch 1, turn; sc in first dc, sc in ea sp and st across: 153 sc.
Row 16: Ch 1, turn; sc in first sc and in ea sc across, change to MC in last sc.
Row 17: Ch 3 [counts as first dc throughout], turn; sk first sc, dc in next sc and in ea sc across: 153 dc.
Rows 18–25: Ch 3, turn; sk first dc, dc in next dc and in ea dc across: 153 dc.
Row 26: Ch 3, turn; sk first dc, dc in next dc and in ea dc across, change to CC in last dc.
Row 27: Ch 1, turn; sc in first dc and in ea dc across: 153 sc.

Row 28: Rep row 16.
Note: Change to larger hook.
Row 29: With larger hook and MC, ch 1, turn; sc in first sc, * sk next sc, 3 dc in next sc, sk next sc, sc in next sc; rep from * across.
Rows 30–98: Rep rows 2–29 twice, then rep rows 2–14 once; fasten off after last row.

Heart (Make 15.)

With larger hook and CC, ch 3.
Row 1 (rs): 2 dc in 3rd ch from hook.
Note: Mark last row as rs.
Row 2: Ch 3, turn; 2 dc in same st, sc in next dc, 3 dc in top of beg ch-3.
Row 3: Ch 3, turn; 2 dc in same st, sc in next dc, sk next dc,

Project was stitched with Jamie Pompadour: White #200 and Pink #201.

3 dc in next sc, sk next dc, sc in next dc, 3 dc in top of tch.

Row 4: Ch 3, turn; sk first dc, sc in next dc, (sk next dc, 3 dc in next sc, sk next dc, sc in next dc) twice, dc in top of tch.

Row 5: Ch 1, turn; sc in first dc, (3 dc in next sc, sk next dc, sc in next dc, sk next dc) twice, 3 dc in next sc, sc in top of tch.

Row 6: Ch 3, turn; dc in first sc, sk next dc, sc in next dc, sk next dc, 3 dc in next sc, sk next dc, sc in next dc; leave rem 6 sts unworked.

Row 7: Ch 2, turn; sk first sc, sk next dc, sc in next dc, sk next dc, 3 dc in next sc, sk next dc, sc in top of tch.

Row 8: Ch 3, turn; sk first sc, sk next dc, sc in next dc, sk next dc, 3 dc in next sc, sc in top of tch; fasten off.

Row 9 (ws): With ws facing, join CC to first unworked st of row 6 with sl st, ch 1, sc in same st, sk next dc, 3 dc in next sc, sk next dc, sc in next dc, sk next dc, 2 dc in last sc.

Row 10: Ch 1, turn; sc in first dc, sk next dc, 3 dc in next sc, sk next dc, sc in next dc, sk next dc, dc in last sc.

Row 11: Ch 1, turn; sc in first dc, 3 dc in next sc, sk next dc, sc in next dc, sk next dc, dc in last sc; fasten off.

Edging

With rs facing, join CC to beg ch with sl st, ch 3, sl st in end of next row, (ch 3, sl st) evenly around; join with sl st to beg sl st; fasten off.

Assembly

Referring to photo for placement, sew 5 Hearts evenly sp in ea dc panel.

Border

Rnd 1 (rs): With smaller hook and rs facing, join CC in top right corner with sl st, ch 1, sc in same st and in ea st across to next corner, 3 sc in corner, * sc evenly across to next corner, 3 sc in corner; rep from * around; join with sl st to beg sc.

Rnd 2 (ws): Ch 1, turn; sc in first sc, * sk next sc, 3 dc in next sc, sk next sc, sc in next sc; rep from * around; join with sl st to beg sc; fasten off.

Rnd 3 (rs): With rs facing, join MC in any sc with sl st, * ch 3, sk next sc, sl st in next dc, ch 3, sk next sc, sl st in next sc; rep from * around; join with sl st to beg sl st; fasten off.

Sparkling Snowflakes

Add dazzle to your holiday decor with a glittering throw. Choose an iridescent yarn to capture glints of light.

Materials

Sportweight acrylic yarn, approximately:
26¼ oz. (2,725 yd.) white
Size G crochet hook or size needed for gauge

Finished Size

Approximately 48" x 64"

Gauge

Ea Snowflake = 8" in diameter

Note: Snowflakes are joined as they are made. Refer to Assembly for directions.

First Snowflake

Ch 8, join with sl st to form ring.
Rnd 1: Hdc in ring, * ch 8, 3 hdc in ring; rep from * 6 times, ch 8, 2 hdc in ring, join with sl st to top of beg hdc: 8 ch-8 sps.
Rnd 2: Sl st in next 4 chs, hdc in ch-8 sp, ch 5, * hdc in same ch-8 sp, ch 5, hdc in next ch-8 sp, ch 5; rep from * around, join with sl st to beg hdc.
Rnd 3: Sl st in next ch-5 sp, (hdc, ch 5, hdc) in same ch-5 sp, (hdc, 4 dc, hdc) in next ch-5 sp [4-dc shell made], * (hdc, ch 5, hdc) in next ch-5 sp, 4-dc shell in next ch-5 sp; rep from * around, join with sl st to beg hdc: 8 4-dc shells.

Rnd 4: Sl st in next ch-5 sp, (hdc, ch 5, hdc) in same ch-5 sp, ch 5, sk next dc, hdc in next dc, ch 5, * (hdc, ch 5, hdc) in next ch-5 sp, ch 5, sk next dc, hdc in next dc, ch 5; rep from * around, join with sl st to beg hdc.
Rnd 5: Sl st in next ch-5 sp, (hdc, ch 5, hdc) in same ch-5 sp, 4-dc shell in next ch-5 sp twice, * (hdc, ch 5, hdc) in next ch-5 sp, 4-dc shell in next ch-5 sp twice; rep from * around, join with sl st to beg hdc: 16 4-dc shells.
Rnd 6: Sl st in next ch-5 sp, (hdc, ch 5, hdc) in same ch-5 sp, ch 5, hdc between next 2 4-dc shells, ch 5, * (hdc, ch 5, hdc) in next ch-5 sp, ch 5, hdc between next 2 4-dc shells, ch 5; rep from * around, join with sl st to beg hdc.
Rnd 7: Sl st in next ch-5 sp, (hdc, ch 5, hdc) in same ch-5 sp, (hdc, 5 dc, hdc) in next ch-5 sp [5-dc shell made], 5-dc shell in next ch-5 sp, * (hdc, ch 5, hdc) in next ch-5 sp, (5-dc shell in next ch-5 sp) twice; rep from * around, join with sl st to beg hdc; fasten off.

Assembly

Afghan is 8 Snowflakes long and 6 Snowflakes wide. Work rem Snowflakes and join as folls:

Second Snowflake of First Row
Rnds 1–6: Work as for First Snowflake.

Rnd 7: Sl st in next ch-5 sp, (hdc, ch 5, hdc) in same ch-5 sp, (5-dc shell in next ch-5 sp) twice, * (hdc, ch 5, hdc) in next ch-5 sp, (5-dc shell in next ch-5 sp) twice; rep from * 5 times; [hdc in next ch-5 sp, ch 2, sl st in corresponding ch-5 sp of last Snowflake, ch 2, hdc in same ch-5 sp of current Snowflake, (5-dc shell in next ch-5 sp) twice] twice, join with sl st to beg hdc; fasten off.

Remaining Snowflakes of First Row
Work as for Second Snowflake of First Row.

First Snowflake of Remaining Rows
Work as for Second Snowflake of First Row.

Remaining Snowflakes of Remaining Rows
Rnds 1–6: Work as for First Snowflake.

Rnd 7: Sl st in next ch-5 sp, (hdc, ch 5, hdc) in same ch-5 sp, (5-dc shell in next ch-5 sp) twice, * (hdc, ch 5, hdc) in next ch-5 sp, (5-dc shell in next ch-5 sp) twice; rep from * 3 times; [hdc in next ch-5 sp, ch 2, sl st in corresponding ch-5 sp of last Snowflake, ch 2, hdc in same ch-5 sp of current Snowflake, (5-dc shell in next ch-5 sp) twice] 4 times, join with sl st to beg hdc; fasten off.

Project was stitched with Glitter Magic: White/Pearl #307.

Double Cross

Friends will actually thank you for double-crossing them with this cozy afghan stitched in single crochet.

Materials
Chunky-weight acrylic yarn,
 approximately:
36 oz. (1,110 yd.) forest green,
 MC
24 oz. (740 yd.) cream, CC
Size K crochet hook or size
 needed for gauge
Yarn needle

Finished Size
Approximately 43" x 52½"

Gauge
Ea Square = 9½"

Note: To change colors, work last
yo of prev st with new color, dropping prev color to ws of work. Use
separate skein CC for ea double
leg of X.

Square (Make 20.)
With MC, ch 26.
Row 1 (rs): With MC, sc in 2nd ch
from hook and in next ch, change
to CC, sc in next 3 chs, change
to MC, sc in next 15 chs, change to
CC, sc in next 3 chs, change to
MC, sc in last 2 chs: 25 sc.
Row 2: With MC, ch 1, turn; sc in
first 3 sc, change to CC, sc in next
3 sc, change to MC, sc in next 13
sc, change to CC, sc in next 3 sc,
change to MC, sc in last 3 sc,
change to CC.
Row 3: With CC, ch 1, turn; sc in
first sc, change to MC, sc in next
3 sc, change to CC, sc in next 3 sc,
change to MC, sc in next 11 sc,

change to CC, sc in next 3 sc,
change to MC, sc in next 3 sc,
change to CC, sc in last sc.
Row 4: With CC, ch 1, turn; sc in
first 2 sc, change to MC, sc in
next 3 sc, change to CC, sc in next
3 sc, change to MC, sc in next
9 sc, change to CC, sc in next 3 sc,
change to MC, sc in next 3 sc,
change to CC, sc in last 2 sc.
Row 5: With CC, ch 1, turn; sc in
first 3 sc, change to MC, sc in
next 3 sc, change to CC, sc in next
3 sc, change to MC, sc in next
7 sc, change to CC, sc in next 3 sc,
change to MC, sc in next 3 sc,
change to CC, sc in last 3 sc, change
to MC.
Rows 6-25: Cont foll *Chart* as est,
reading odd (rs) rows from right
to left and even (ws) rows from
left to right; fasten off after last
row.

Assembly
Afghan is 5 squares long and 4
squares wide. Whipstitch squares
tog.

Chart

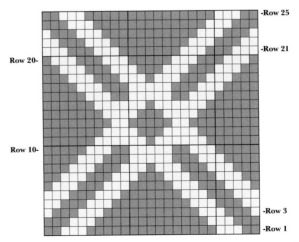

Border
Rnd 1: With rs facing, join MC in
any corner with sl st, ch 1, sc in
same st as joining, sc evenly across
to next corner, * 3 sc in corner,
sc evenly across to next corner;
rep from * around; join with sl st
to beg sc; fasten off.
Rnd 2: With rs facing, join CC in
any corner with sl st, ch 1, sc in
same st as joining, sc evenly across
to next corner, * 3 sc in corner,
sc evenly across to next corner;
rep from * around; join with sl st
to beg sc.
Rnd 3: Ch 1, sc in same st,
sc evenly across to next corner,
* 3 sc in corner, sc evenly across
to next corner; rep from *
around; join with sl st to beg sc.
Rnd 4: Ch 1, sc in same st,
sc evenly across to next corner,
* 3 sc in corner, sc evenly across
to next corner; rep from *
around; join with sl st to beg sc;
fasten off.
Rnd 5: Rep rnd 1.
Rnds 6 and 7: With MC, rep rnd
3 twice.
Rnd 8: Rep rnd 4.

Project stitched in Homespun: Country #304 and Deco #309.

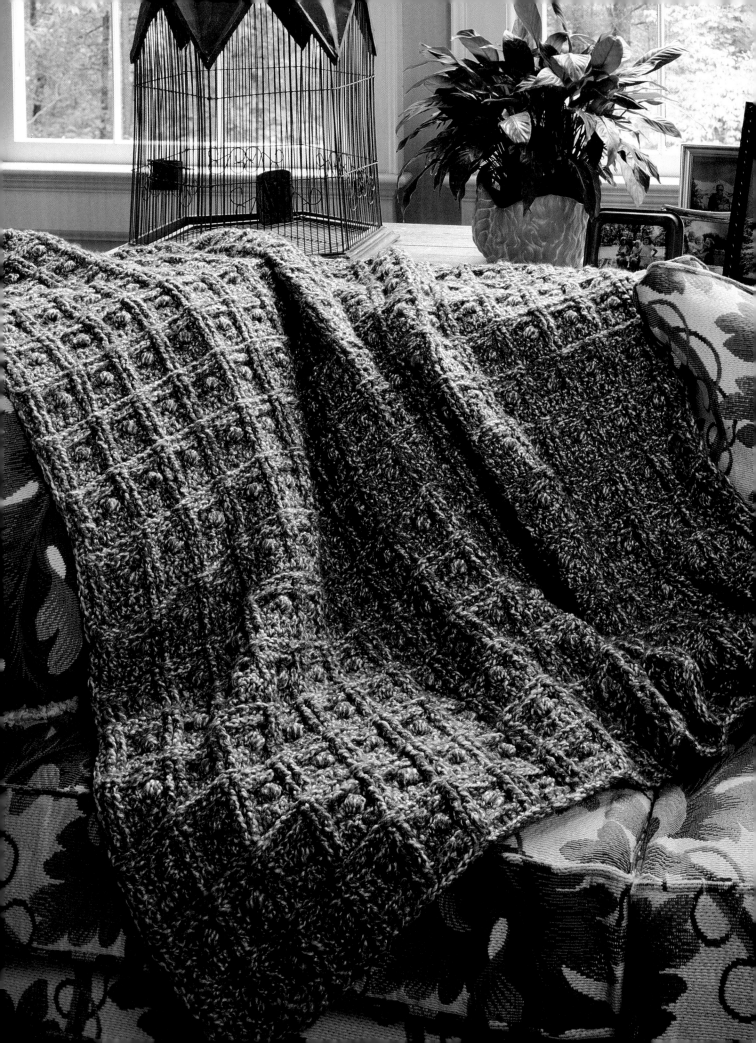

Puffs in Boxes

Stitched in chunky yarn, this densely textured afghan will keep you warm on the coldest nights.

Materials

Chunky-weight acrylic yarn, approximately:
90 oz. (2,775 yd.) brown-and-gray variegated
Sizes J and K crochet hooks or sizes to obtain gauge

Finished Size

Approximately 53" x 54"

Gauge

In pat with larger hook, 11 sts and 8 rows = 4"

Pattern Stitches

Back Post dc (BPdc): Yo, insert hook from back to front around post of st indicated, yo and pull up lp, (yo and pull through 2 lps) twice; sk st behind BPdc.

Front Post dc (FPdc): Yo, insert hook from front to back around post of st indicated, yo and pull up lp, (yo and pull through 2 lps) twice; sk st behind FPdc.

Puff: (Yo, insert hook in st indicated, yo and pull up lp) 5 times, yo and pull through all 11 lps on hook.

With larger hook, ch 146.
Row 1 (rs): Dc in 4th ch from hook and in ea ch across: 144 dc.
Row 2: Ch 2 [counts as first hdc throughout], turn; sk first dc, (BPdc around next 2 dc, FPdc around next 5 FPdc) across to last 2 dc, BPdc around last 2 dc, hdc in top of tch.

Row 3: Ch 2, turn; sk first hdc, (FPdc around next 2 BPdc, hdc in next 5 FPdc) across to last 2 BPdc, FPdc around last 2 BPdc, hdc in top of tch.
Row 4: Ch 2, turn; sk first hdc, * BPdc around next 2 FPdc, sc in next 2 hdc, puff in next hdc, sc in next 2 hdc; rep from * across to last 2 FPdc, BPdc around last 2 FPdc, hdc in top of tch.
Row 5: Ch 2, turn; sk first hdc, (FPdc around next 2 BPdc, dc in next 5 sts) across to last 2 BPdc, FPdc around last 2 BPdc, hdc in top of tch.
Row 6: Ch 2, turn; sk first hdc, (BPdc around next 2 FPdc, FPdc around next 5 dc) across to last 2 FPdc, BPdc around last 2 FPdc, hdc in top of tch.

Row 7: Ch 2, turn; BPdc around ea st across, hdc in top of tch.
Row 8: Ch 2, turn; sk first hdc, (BPdc around next 2 BPdc, dc in next 5 BPdc) across to last 2 BPdc, BPdc around last 2 BPdc, hdc in top of tch.
Rows 9-109: Rep rows 3-8, 16 times, then rep rows 3-7 once; do not fasten off.

Border

With smaller hook, ch 1, 3 sc in same st, sc evenly across left side to next corner, 3 sc in corner, sl st evenly across to next corner, 3 sc in corner, sc evenly across to next corner, 3 sc in corner, sl st evenly across to next corner; join with sl st to beg sc; fasten off.

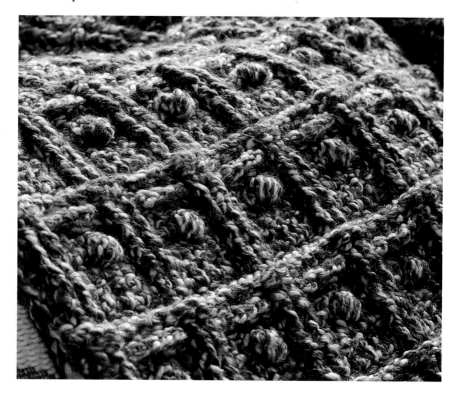

Project was stitched with Homespun: Shaker #301.

Granny's Diamonds

Set granny squares on point for this gem of an afghan. Finish it with a twisted chain border.

Materials
Worsted-weight acrylic yarn, approximately:
12 oz. (600 yd.) light blue, MC
12 oz. (600 yd.) light yellow, A
12 oz. (600 yd.) white, B
Size K crochet hook or size to obtain gauge
Yarn needle

Finished Size
Approximately 41" x 47½"

Gauge
Ea Square = 6½"

Square (Make 42.)

Center
With MC, ch 4, join with sl st to form ring.
Rnd 1 (rs): Ch 3 [counts as first dc throughout], 2 dc in ring, (ch 3, 3 dc in ring) 3 times, ch 3; join with sl st to top of beg ch-3.
Note: Mark last rnd as rs.
Rnd 2: Sl st in first 2 dc, sl st in first ch-3 sp, (ch 3, 2 dc, ch 3, 3 dc) in same ch-3 sp, * ch 2, (3 dc, ch 3, 3 dc) in next ch-3 sp; rep from * twice, ch 2; join with sl st to top of beg ch-3.
Rnd 3: Sl st in first 2 dc, sl st in first ch-3 sp, (ch 3, 2 dc, ch 3, 3 dc) in same ch-3 sp, * ch 2, 3 dc in next ch-2 sp, ch 2, (3 dc, ch 3, 3 dc) in next ch-3 sp; rep from * twice, ch 2, 3 dc in next sp, ch 2; join with sl st to top of beg ch-3; fasten off.

First Corner
Row 1 (rs): With rs facing, join A in any ch-3 sp with sl st, ch 1, work 13 sc evenly sp across edge to next ch-3 sp: 13 sc.
Rows 2–7: Ch 1, turn; sk first sc, sc in ea sc across to last sc, sk last sc.
Row 8: Ch 1, turn; sl st to first sc; fasten off.

Second Corner
Row 1 (rs): With rs facing, join B in next ch-3 sp with sl st, ch 1, work 13 sc evenly sp across edge to next ch-3 sp: 13 sc.
Rows 2–8: Work as for rows 2–8 of First Corner.

Third Corner
Row 1 (rs): With rs facing, join A in next ch-3 sp with sl st, ch 1, work 13 sc evenly sp across edge to next ch-3 sp: 13 sc.
Rows 2–8: Work as for rows 2–8 of First Corner.

Fourth Corner
Work as for Second Corner.

Assembly
Afghan is 7 squares long and 6 squares wide. Whipstitch squares tog.

Border
Rnd 1 (rs): With rs facing, join MC in top right corner with sl st, ch 1, * work 137 sc evenly sp across to next corner, 3 sc in corner, work 161 sc evenly sp across to next corner, work 3 sc in corner; rep from * around; join with sl st to beg sc: 608 sc.
Rnd 2 (ws): Ch 1, turn; sc in first sc and in ea sc across to corner, * 3 sc in corner, sc in ea sc across to next corner; rep from * around; join with sl st to beg sc; fasten off: 616 sc.
Rnd 3: With rs facing, join A in any corner with sl st, ch 1, sc in same st as joining, * ch 3, sk 2 sc, sc in next sc; rep from * around; join with sl st to beg sc; fasten off.
Rnd 4: With rs facing, join B in corner sc with sl st, ch 1, sc in same st as joining, * ch 3, drop lp from hook, insert hook in ch-3 sp on rnd 3, pick up dropped lp, yo and pull through lp; rep from * around; join with sl st to beg sc; fasten off.

Project was stitched with Jamie 4 Ply: Pastel Blue #106, Pastel Yellow #157, and White #100.

Great Gingham

Basic checks are beautiful when stitched in luscious yarn. Choose flecked yarn in coordinating colors for a rich look.

Materials

Chunky-weight acrylic yarn, approximately:
48 oz. (1,480 yd.) navy-and-rose variegated, MC
30 oz. (925 yd.) forest green, A
18 oz. (555 yd.) dark rose, B
Size J crochet hook or size to obtain gauge
Yarn needle

Finished Size

Approximately 55" x 73"

Gauge

In pat, 16 sts and 11 rows = 6"

Note: To change colors, work last yo of prev st with new color, dropping prev color to ws of work. Do not carry yarn across row.

Strip 1 (Make 5.)

With A, ch 16.
Row 1 (rs): (Sc, dc) in 2nd ch from hook, * sk 1 ch, (sc, dc) in next ch; rep from * across: 16 sts.
Note: Mark last row as rs.
Rows 2–11: Ch 1, turn; (sc, dc) in first dc, * sk next sc, (sc, dc) in next dc; rep from * across, sk last sc.

Row 12: Ch 1, turn; (sc, dc) in first dc, * sk next sc, (sc, dc) in next dc; rep from * across, change to MC, sk last sc.
Rows 13–23: With MC, rep row 2, 11 times.
Row 24: Ch 1, turn; (sc, dc) in first dc, * sk next sc, (sc, dc) in next dc; rep from * across, change to A, sk last sc.
Rows 25–35: With A, rep row 2, 11 times.
Row 36: Rep row 12.
Rows 37–132: Rep rows 13–36, 4 times; fasten off after last row.

Strip 2 (Make 4.)

With MC, ch 16.
Row 1 (rs): (Sc, dc) in 2nd ch from hook, * sk 1 ch, (sc, dc) in next ch; rep from * across: 16 sts.
Note: Mark last row as rs.
Rows 2–11: Ch 1, turn; (sc, dc) in first dc, * sk next sc, (sc, dc) in next dc; rep from * across, sk last sc.
Row 12: Ch 1, turn; (sc, dc) in first dc, * sk next sc, (sc, dc) in next dc; rep from * across, change to B, sk last sc.
Rows 13–23: With B, rep row 2, 11 times.
Row 24: Ch 1, turn; (sc, dc) in first dc, * sk next sc, (sc, dc) in

next dc; rep from * across, change to MC, sk last sc.
Rows 25–35: With MC, rep row 2, 11 times.
Row 36: Rep row 12.
Rows 37–132: Rep rows 13–36, 4 times; fasten off after last row.

Assembly

Beg and ending with Strip 1, and alternating Strip 1 and Strip 2, whipstitch Strips tog.

Border

Rnd 1 (rs): With rs facing, join MC to top right corner with sl st, sc in same st, (sc in next dc, dc in next sc) across to next corner, 2 sc in corner, (sc, dc) evenly across to next corner, 2 sc in corner, sc evenly across to next corner, 2 sc in corner, (sc, dc) evenly across to next corner; join with sl st to beg sc.
Rnd 2: Ch 1, turn; sc in ea st across to next corner, * 2 sc in corner, sc in ea st across to next corner; rep from * around; join with sl st to beg sc; fasten off.

Project was stitched with Homespun: Country #304, Antique #307, and Mission #303.

General Directions

Crochet Abbreviations

beg	begin(ning)	ft lp(s)	front loop(s)	st(s)	stitch(es)
bet	between	grp(s)	group(s)	tch	turning chain
bk lp(s)	back loop(s)	hdc	half double crochet	tog	together
ch	chain(s)	inc	increas(es) (ed) (ing)	tr	triple crochet
ch-	refers to chain	lp(s)	loop(s)	yo	yarn over
	previously made	pat(s)	pattern(s)		
cl	cluster(s)	prev	previous		
cont	continu(e) (ing)	rem	remain(s) (ing)		
dc	double crochet	rep	repeat(s)		
dec	decreas(es) (ed) (ing)	rnd(s)	round(s)		
dtr	double triple crochet	sc	single crochet		
ea	each	sk	skip(ped)		
est	established	sl st	slip stitch		
foll	follow(s) (ing)	sp(s)	space(s)		

Repeat whatever follows * as indicated. "Rep from * 3 times more" means to work 4 times in all.

Work directions given in parentheses ( ) and brackets [ ] the number of times specified or in the place specified.

Aluminum Crochet Hook Sizes

U.S.	Size	Metric	Canada/U.K.	U.S.	Size	Metric	Canada/U.K.
B	(1)	2.25	13	H	(8)	5.00	6
C	(2)	2.75		I	(9)	5.50	5
D	(3)	3.25	10	J	(10)	6.00	4
E	(4)	3.50	9	K	(10½)	6.50	3
F	(5)	4.00		N		10.00	000
G	(6)	4.25	8				

Metric Conversion
Common Measures

⅛" = 3 mm	5" = 12.7 cm	⅛ yard = 0.11 m
¼" = 6 mm	6" = 15.2 cm	¼ yard = 0.23 m
⅜" = 9 mm	7" = 17.8 cm	⅓ yard = 0.3 m
½" = 1.3 cm	8" = 20.3 cm	⅜ yard = 0.34 m
⅝" = 1.6 cm	9" = 22.9 cm	½ yard = 0.46 m
¾" = 1.9 cm	10" = 25.4 cm	⅝ yard = 0.57 m
⅞" = 2.2 cm	11" = 27.9 cm	⅔ yard = 0.61 m
1" = 2.5 cm	12" = 30.5 cm	¾ yard = 0.69 m
2" = 5.1 cm	36" = 91.5 cm	⅞ yard = 0.8 m
3" = 7.6 cm	45" = 114.3 cm	1 yard = 0.91 m
4" = 10.2 cm	60" = 152.4 cm	

A Note to Left-Handed Crocheters

Since instructions for crocheted projects most often appear with right-handed instructions only, it may be worth your while to learn right-handed crochet techniques. Since the work is shared between the hands in crochet, it may be surprisingly easy for you to make use of the accompanying diagrams. If working in this way is not comfortable, use a mirror to reverse the diagrams or reverse them on a photocopier.

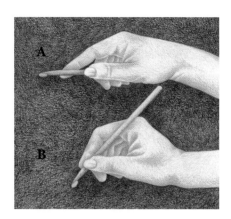

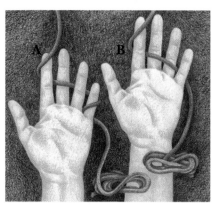

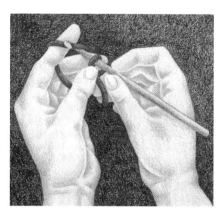

Holding the Hook

Hold the hook as you would a piece of chalk (**A**) or a pencil (**B**). If your hook has a finger rest, position your thumb and opposing finger there for extra control.

Holding the Yarn

Weave the yarn through the fingers of your left hand. Some people like to wrap the yarn around the little finger for extra control (**A**); some do not (**B**). In either case, the forefinger plays the most important role in regulating tension as yarn is fed into the work.

Working Together

Once work has begun, the thumb and the middle finger of the left hand come into play, pressing together to hold the stitches just made.

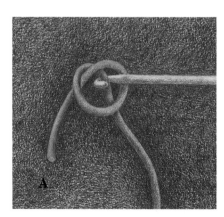

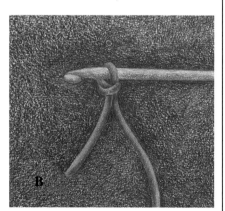

Gauge

Before beginning a project, work a 4"-square gauge swatch, using the recommended size hook. Count and compare the number of stitches per inch in the swatch with the designer's gauge. If you have fewer stitches in your swatch, try a smaller hook; if you have more stitches, try a larger hook.

Slip Knot

A. Loop the yarn around and let the loose end of the yarn fall behind the loop to form a pretzel shape as shown. Insert the hook.

B. Pull both ends to close the knot.

Chain Stitch

A. Place slip knot on hook. With thumb and middle finger of left hand holding yarn end, wrap yarn up and over hook (from back to front). This movement is called "yarn over (yo)" and is basic to every crochet stitch.

B. Use hook to pull yarn through loop (lp) already on hook. Combination of yo and pulling yarn through lp makes 1 chain stitch (ch).

C. Repeat A and B until ch is desired length. Try to keep movements even and relaxed and all ch stitches (sts) same size. Hold ch near working area to keep it from twisting. Count sts as shown in diagram. (Do not count lp on hook or slip knot.)

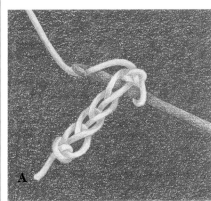

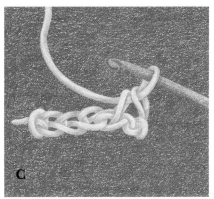

Slip Stitch

Here slip stitch (sl st) is used to join ring. Taking care not to twist chain, insert hook into first ch made, yo and pull through ch and lp on hook (sl st made). Sl st can also be used to join finished pieces or to move across groups of sts without adding height to work.

Single Crochet

A. Insert hook under top 2 lps of 2nd ch from hook and yo. (Always work sts through top 2 lps unless directions specify otherwise.)
B. Yo and pull yarn through ch (2 lps on hook).
C. Yo and pull yarn through 2 lps on hook (1 sc made).

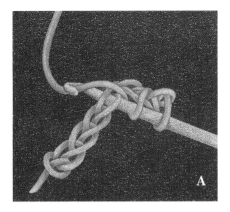

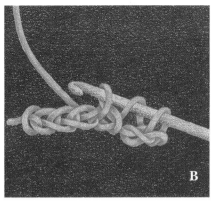

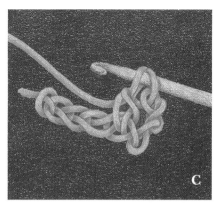

Double Crochet

A. Yo, insert hook into 4th ch from hook, and yo.
B. Yo and pull yarn through ch (3 lps on hook).

C. Yo and pull through 2 lps on hook (2 lps remaining).
D. Yo and pull through 2 remaining (rem) lps (1 dc made).

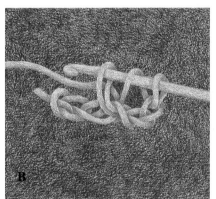

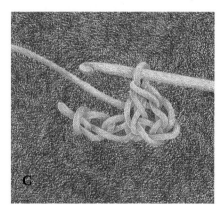

Half Double Crochet

A. Yo and insert hook into 3rd ch from hook.

B. Yo and pull through ch (3 lps on hook).

C. Yo and pull yarn through all 3 lps on hook (1 hdc made).

Triple Crochet

A. Yo twice, insert hook into 5th ch from hook. Yo and pull through ch (4 lps on hook).
B. Yo and pull through 2 lps on hook (3 lps rem). Yo and pull through 2 lps on hook (2 lps rem). Yo and pull through 2 lps on hook (1 tr made).

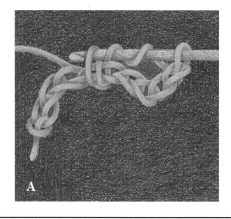

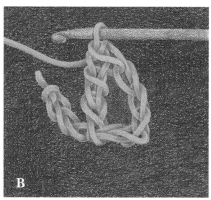

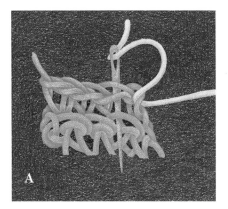

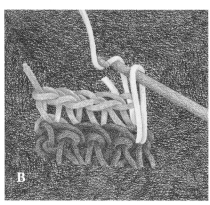

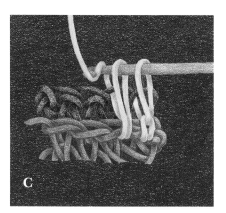

Assembly

To assemble crocheted pieces, use a large-eyed yarn needle to whipstitch (**A**) or a crochet hook to slip stitch (**B**) the pieces together. Pieces can also be joined using single crochet stitches (**C**), but this makes a heavier seam.

When making squares or other pieces to be stitched together, leave a 20" tail of yarn when fastening off. This yarn tail can then be used to stitch the pieces together, with all stitches and rows of the squares or the strips aligned and running in the same direction.

Joining Yarn

To change colors or to begin a new skein of yarn at the end of a row, work the last yarn over for the last stitch of the previous row with the new yarn.

Fastening Off

Cut the yarn, leaving a 6" tail. Yarn over and pull the tail through the last loop on the hook. Thread the tail into a large-eyed yarn needle and weave it carefully into the back of the work.

Metric Math

When you know:	Multiply by:	To find:	When you know:	Multiply by:	To find:
inches (")	25	millimeters (mm)	millimeters (mm)	0.039	inches (")
inches (")	2.5	centimeters (cm)	centimeters (cm)	0.39	inches (")
inches (")	0.025	meters (m)	meters (m)	39	inches (")
yards (yd.)	0.9	meters (m)	meters (m)	1.093	yards (yd.)
ounces (oz.)	28.35	grams (g)	grams (g)	0.035	ounces (oz.)

Loop Stitch (lp st)

A. With wrong side (ws) of work facing, insert hook in next st. Wrap yarn over ruler or index finger to form 1"-high lp. Pick up bottom strand of yarn with hook and pull through st, keeping lp taut.

B. Yo and pull through both lps on hook to complete st as a sc.

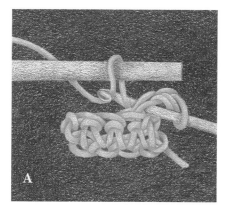

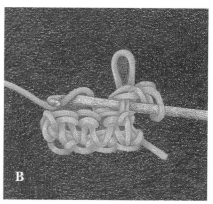

Front Post dc (FPdc)

A. Yo and insert hook from front to back around post of st on previous row.

B. Complete dc st as usual. (Back post dc [BPdc] is worked in same manner, except you insert hook from back to front around post.)

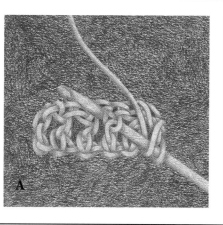

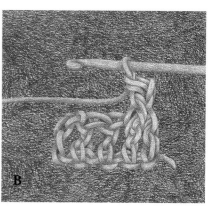

Basic Popcorn

A. Work 5 dc in st indicated, drop lp from hook, and insert hook in first dc of 5-dc grp.

B. Pick up dropped lp and pull through.

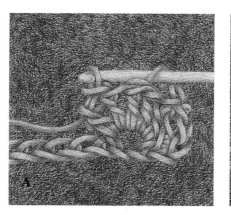

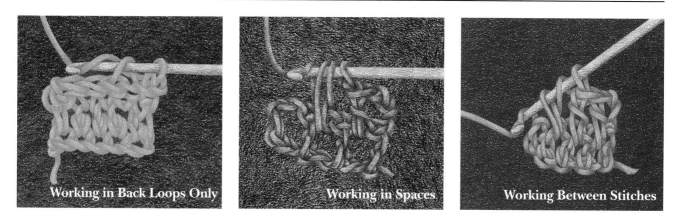

Working in Back Loops Only

Working in Spaces

Working Between Stitches

Stitch Placement Variations

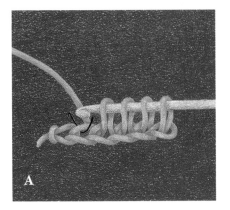

A

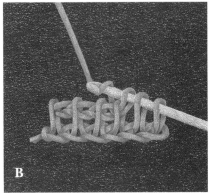

B

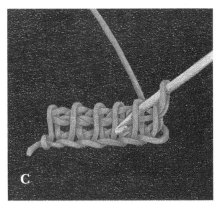

C

Afghan Stitch

A. *Row 1: Step 1:* Keeping all lps on hook, pull up lp through top lp only in 2nd ch from hook and in ea ch across = same number of lps and chs. Do not turn.

B. *Step 2:* Yo and pull through first lp on hook, * yo and pull through 2 lps on hook, rep from * across (1 lp rem on hook for first lp of next row). Do not turn.

C. *Row 2: Step 1:* Keeping all lps on hook, pull up lp from under 2nd vertical bar, * pull up lp from under next vertical bar, rep from * across. Do not turn. *Step 2:* Rep step 2 of row 1.

Rep both steps of row 2 for required number of rows. Fasten off after last row by working sl st in ea bar across.

D. Finished fabric is perfect grid for cross-stitch.

D

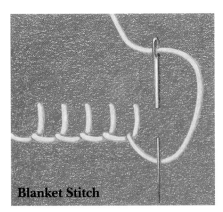

Blanket Stitch

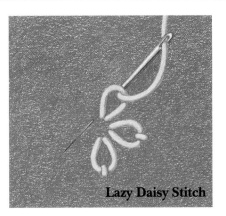

Lazy Daisy Stitch

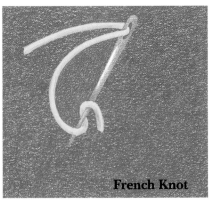

French Knot

Embroidery Stitches

Thread a large-eyed yarn needle to embellish a crocheted piece with embroidery. Weave in the yarn tails; do not use knots.

Fringe

To make a simple fringe, cut the required number of yarn lengths as specified in the directions.

Insert the hook through 1 stitch at the edge of the afghan and fold the yarn lengths in half over the hook (**A**). Pull the folded yarn partway through the stitch to form a loop (**B**). Pull the yarn ends through the loop (**C**) and pull tight (**D**).

Tassel

Wrap the yarn around a piece of cardboard as specified in the directions. At 1 end, slip a 5" yarn length under the loops and knot tightly. Cut the loops at other end (**A**). Loop and tightly wrap a 36" yarn length around the tassel (**B**). Secure the yarn ends and tuck them into the tassel.

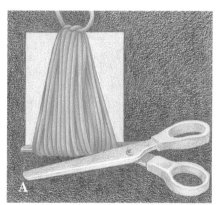

Lion Brand® Yarns

Al•Pa•Ka (Article #740)
Worsted-weight yarn
30% alpaka, 30% wool,
   40% acrylic
1¾ oz. (107 yd.) balls

Fishermen's Wool (Article #150)
Worsted-weight yarn
100% wool
8 oz. (465 yd.) skeins

Glitter Magic (Article #350)
Sportweight yarn
95% acrylic, 5% polyester wrap
8¾ oz. (907 yd.) balls

Homespun (Article #790)
Chunky-weight yarn
98% acrylic, 2% polyester
6 oz. (185 yd.) skeins

Imagine (Article #780)
Worsted-weight yarn
80% acrylic, 20% mohair
Solids: 2½ oz. (222 yd.) balls
Multicolors: 2 oz. (179 yd.) balls

Jamie® Baby (Article #870)
Sportweight yarn
100% Monsanto acrylic with
   Bounce-Back® fibers
Solids: 1¾ oz. (196 yd.) skeins
Multicolors: 1½ oz. (170 yd.) skeins

Jamie 4 Ply (Article #810)
Worsted-weight yarn
100% Monsanto acrylic with
   Bounce-Back® fibers
Solids: 6 oz. (300 yd.) skeins

Jamie® Pompadour (Article #890)
Sportweight yarn
85% Monsanto acrylic with
   Bounce-Back® fibers, 15% rayon
   wrap
Solids: 1¾ oz. (196 yd.) skeins

Jiffy® (Article #450)
Chunky-weight brushed acrylic
   yarn
100% Monsanto acrylic with
   Bounce-Back® fibers
Solids: 3 oz. (135 yd.) balls
Multicolors: 2½ oz. (115 yd.) balls

Keepsake® Sayelle (Article #610)
Worsted-weight yarn
100% Monsanto acrylic with
   Bounce-Back® fibers
Solids: 6 oz. (312 yd.) skeins
Multicolors: 5 oz. (260 yd.) skeins

Kitchen Cotton (Article #760)
Worsted-weight yarn
100% cotton
Solids: 5 oz. (236 yd.) balls
Multicolors: 4 oz. (189 yd.) balls

Lion Chenille (Article #710) and
Chenille Sensations (Article #730)
Worsted-weight yarn
100% Monsanto acrylic
1.4 oz. (87 yd.) skeins

Wool-Ease® (Article #620)
Worsted-weight yarn
Solids and heathers: 80% acrylic,
   20% wool
Multicolors: 78% acrylic, 19%
   wool, 3% polyester
Sprinkles: 86% acrylic, 10% wool,
   4% viscose
Frosts: 70% acrylic, 20% wool, 10%
   polyamide
Solids, heathers, and sprinkles:
   3 oz. (197 yd.) balls
Multicolors and frosts: 2½ oz.
   (162 yd.) balls

Ordering Information

Lion Brand Yarn is widely available in retail stores across the country. If you are unable to find Lion Brand Yarn locally, you may order it by calling 1-800-258-9276 (YARN).

Photographs

Ralph Anderson: Front cover, 1, 6, 7, 12, 13, 18, 19, 24, 25, 30, 31, 36, 37, 42, 43, 50, 51, 55–57, 62, 63, 67, 69, 72, 73, 80, 87, 88, 92, 93, 99, 105, 114–116, 121, 135.

Keith Harrelson: 9–11, 14, 16, 17, 21, 22, 26–29, 32–35, 39, 40, 45, 47–49, 53, 54, 58–61, 65, 70, 71, 75–78, 83, 89, 90, 94–97, 101, 102, 106–109, 111, 112, 117, 118, 123, 124 , 126, 129–131, 133.

John O'Hagan: 41.

Special Thanks

Andrea Anderson
Dana Basinger
Lew and Suzie Burdette
John and Jane George
Paul and Jo Harris
Alan and Cecilia Matthews
Mark McCowan
Katie Beth Pickering
Wanda Salmon
Barbara Stone
Richard Tubb